D1705012

JULIUS CAESAR

Other Works by Christopher Andrews

TRIUMVIRATE SERIES

Pandora's Game
The Darkness Within
(collection)
Of Wolf and Man
(Bronze IPPY winner for Horror)
Araknid

PARANORMALS SERIES

Paranormals
Paranormals: We Are Not Alone
Paranormals: Darkness Reigns

NOVELIZATIONS

Dream Parlor
Hamlet: Prince of Denmark
Night of the Living Dead
Macbeth

SCREENPLAYS

Thirst
Dream Parlor
(written with Jonathan Lawrence)
Mistake
Vale Todo / Anything Goes
(written with Roberto Estrella)

WEB SERIES

Duet

VIDEO GAMES

Bankjob

JULIUS CAESAR

A Novelization by

CHRISTOPHER ANDREWS

Adapted from the play

The Tragedy of Julius Caesar

by

WILLIAM SHAKESPEARE

Rising Star Visionary Press hardcover edition: November, 2022

A Rising Star Visionary Press book
for extra copies please contact by e-mail at
risingstarvisionarypress@earthlink.net
or send by regular mail to
Rising Star Visionary Press
Copies Department
P O Box 9226
Fountain Valley, CA 92728-9226

For my wife, editor, and Imzadi,
Yvonne Isaak-Andrews,
without whom these works would not exist.

For my mother,
Lynda Andrews,
whose adversity in understanding
Shakespeare inspired this journey.

And for my daughter,
Arianna Kristina Andrews,
hoping she'll find these books helpful
as she continues her scholastic career.

WHY NOVELIZE *JULIUS CAESAR*?

A FOREWORD BY THE AUTHOR

My original inspiration for novelizing Shakespeare's works stemmed from my being cast in the role of Hamlet for a 1992 stage production of Tom Stoppard's *Rosencrantz and Guildenstern Are Dead*, wherein Stoppard took two minor characters from *Hamlet* and allowed the story to unfold from their point of view.

Before the play debuted, I told my parents that they would need to know *Hamlet* in order to appreciate the production, but they – especially my mother – insisted they could not understand Shakespeare's language. To assist them with this hindrance, I rented Franco Zeffirelli's film version of *Hamlet* and watched it with them, "translating" the dialogue along the way.

To my delight, I discovered that, as the movie played on, I had to do it less and less; they started "getting it." All it took was that nudge, getting them past the *intimidation* of Shakespeare, and they – particularly my mother – enjoyed the story.

How many others like my mother were out there? How many would savor Shakespeare's works if they just had a little help?

My novelization *Hamlet: Prince of Denmark* was released in 2005, followed by *Macbeth* in 2015, and the reader response has been so positive, I decided to press onward. Hence ... my novelization of Shakespeare's *Julius Caesar*.

As with *Hamlet* and *Macbeth*, I approached the source material with two goals:

(1) I wanted to "translate" the language as little as possible, merely prodding the words a bit here and there. Sometimes this involved updating archaic terms because their original syntax has

been lost. Other passages required additional text to clarify jargon that was familiar in Shakespeare's time; Shakespeare referenced myths or folklore that were common knowledge then, but required more explanation for the modern reader.

But more often than not, I discovered that flipping the subject/verb agreement or adjusting what today feels like a misplaced modifier was all that was necessary to make a given passage clearer. And some text required no alteration whatsoever – once the preceding and following dialogue were clarified, the original verbiage made perfect sense with no further help from me.

(2) I would elaborate within the prose as to what each character might be doing/thinking/feeling at any given point. Thus, the dialogue would again become understandable, as the reader would now have improved context for what was being said. When it came to executing, say, Mark Antony's "performance," sometimes I borrowed from Marlon Brando or Charlton Heston or Robert Stephens, and other times I came up with something entirely on my own.

It is all a matter of interpretation. Given Shakespeare's minimal stage directions, there are few absolutes as to how any given line should be delivered. Each actor brings something special to the role; each director has their unique vision. By "acting out the story" as it were, I hope to convey what it would be like to see *Julius Caesar* performed, allowing the reader to better grasp, and therefore enjoy, the experience.

With each of Shakespeare's plays, I encounter different "curve balls" which I must address; in *Macbeth*, for instance, different editions disagree on how some Scenes were attached to the various Acts. For *Julius Caesar*, I found a greater number of conflicting definitions for the play's dated lexicon. For example, one edition suggested that Brutus' use of "secret" in his orchard meant *discreet* ... but another edition insisted that "secret" actually meant *resolute*. So I ultimately had to use my own judgment – my own interpretations, as it were.

And so, here is my interpretation of *The Tragedy of Julius Caesar*. I hope you will find Shakespeare's rich language easier to understand, but as with my adaptations of the Melancholy Dane and the Scottish Play, I *am* asking you to put on your Thinking Caps – this is still Shakespeare; I'm just sitting alongside you, as I did my parents in 1992. I've tweaked, rearranged, adjusted ... but wherever possible, I've left the dialogue completely unaltered.

In this way, I hope to help you better enjoy the work of The Bard as well.

Christopher Andrews
August, 2022

DRAMATIS PERSONAE

JULIUS CAESAR, Roman statesman and general

OCTAVIUS CAESAR

MARK ANTONY } Triumvirs after Julius Caesar

MARCUS AEMILIUS LEPIDUS

CICERO

PUBLIUS } Senators

POPILIUS LENA

MARCUS BRUTUS, Leader of the conspiracy against Julius Caesar

CAIUS CASSIUS

CASCA

TREBONIUS

CAIUS LIGARIUS } Conspirators against Julius Caesar

DECIUS BRUTUS

METELLUS CIMBER

CINNA

FLAVIUS and MURELLUS, Tribunes

ARTEMIDORUS of Cnidos, a Teacher of rhetoric

A SOOTHSAYER

CINNA, a Poet

Another POET

LUCILIUS

TITINIUS

MESSALA   } Friends to Brutus and Cassius

Young CATO

VOLUMNIUS

VARRUS

CLITUS

CLAUDIO   } Servants to Brutus

STRATO

LUCIUS

DARDANIUS

PINDARUS, Servant to Cassius

CALPHURNIA, Wife to Caesar

PORTIA, Wife to Brutus

COMMONERS or PLEBEIANS, SENATORS, GUARDS or SOLDIERS, ATTENDANTS, etc.

LOCATIONS

ROME; encampment near SARDIS; plains near PHILIPPI

PART ONE

CHAPTER ONE

Surrounded by reveling, screaming plebeians of the lowest order, Flavius and Murellus – two Tribunes of the Roman Republic – attempted to traverse the streets of Rome.

The dirty throng jumped about and cheered and wailed like raving lunatics, bewildering in their unwarranted gallivanting. One woman, her robes sagging away from her breasts in deplorable fashion, stumbled and actually latched onto Flavius' forearm for balance; the Tribune shook free of the commoner and raised his hand to strike her for her impertinence, but she danced her drunken self away before he could deliver just punishment.

By the gods, what was going on this day? What mayhem was this? The Feast of Lupercal was a pastoral festival to promote health and fertility, one of purification and expiation – *not* an excuse to indulge every crude whim or hedonistic impulse!

Flavius and Murellus exchanged a wordless communion of disgust and bewilderment at the whole state of affairs, then something caught Murellus' eye; his face twisted as he gestured. Flavius followed his gaze, and his own expression soured as though he had bitten into a too-ripe lemon.

Centered within the upcoming juncture of several streets rose a marble bust of Julius Caesar, that worrisome Roman statesman, general, and now *Dictator Perpetuo* – Dictator for Life – of the Roman Republic. As though "dictator for life" were somehow compatible with *any* "republic."

Adding salt to the wound, said bust of Caesar had been decorated with wreath upon wreath of flowers, so many that the facsimile of his robes of office were buried from sight. And one wreath in particular rested upon the head of the bust, looking for all the world like a royal crown.

The commoners caroused, but Flavius and Murellus seethed.

At that moment, a cluster of such commoners burst into an especially reprehensible round of laughter, accompanied by applause and more carrying about. One of them threw a skin of wine into the air, and all laughed harder still as the wasted ambrosia rained upon them.

Flavius could take no more.

Rushing forward, he forced himself amongst them, shouting, "Go hence! Home, you idle creatures, get you home!"

The crowd regarded him, observed his robes of office, and appeared unimpressed.

"Is this a holiday?" Flavius demanded. "What, do you not know – being of the laboring class – that you ought not walk about upon a laboring day without the garb and tools of your profession?"

This prompted the plebeians to further laughter and rolling their collective eyes. A "laboring day," did he say? By the gods, it was the Feast of Lupercal! Surely this Tribune of Rome spoke in jest.

Flavius singled out one man in particular. "Speak, what trade are you?"

The man chuckled, his gap-toothed grin as vacuous as his eyes; he appeared to feel this must be some game. "Why, sir, a carpenter."

Murellus joined his fellow Tribune in challenging, "Where is your leather apron and your ruler? What are you doing with your best apparel on?"

The self-proclaimed carpenter continued chuckling as he glanced down at his nicest robes, but he looked a bit less certain of his circumstances.

Murellus turned upon another man. "You, sir, what trade are you?"

The shorter, bearded man smirked – a brazen expression that pleased neither Murellus nor Flavius in the slightest – and answered, "Truly, sir, in comparison with a fine workman, I am but, as you would say ... a cobbler."

The man spoke as though making some sort of joke; was he speaking literally, or not? Frustrated, Murellus sneered, "But what *trade* are you? Answer me directly."

The man maintained his insipid smirk, his eyes dancing about the faces of his companions as he said, "A trade, sir, that I hope I may use with a safe conscience, which is indeed, sir, a mender ... of bad *soles*." He followed this with an audacious wink to the carpenter, which prompted further laughter from all but the two baffled Tribunes.

Damn it, had the fool meant "soles," or "souls"? Was he incapable of plain and direct speech? Flavius clapped his hands before the bearded man's face and demanded, "What *trade*, you knave? You naughty knave, what *trade*?"

But this "cobbler," if that's what he truly was, remained unimpressed by Flavius' station and his anger. "No, I beseech you, sir, do not be out of temper with me." The ornery twinkle in his eyes grew further as he stared pointedly down at Murellus' feet. "Yet if you be out, sir, I can mend you."

More laughter from the crowd, more offense taken by the Tribunes.

Murellus seized the bearded man's arm. "What do you mean by that? 'Mend me,' you saucy fellow?"

The bearded man blinked down at the hand that held him, and his reply was a touch confused, as though he could not understand why Murellus did not appreciate his humor. "Why, sir, cobble you."

Flavius snapped, "You *are* a cobbler, are you?"

The cobbler eased his arm out of Murellus' grip, and his tone reclaimed some of its jovial attitude. "Truly, sir, all that I live by is with the awl. I meddle with no tradesman's matters nor women's matters, but *withal* ..." He grinned at the crowd over his pun on "with awl," and everyone – save the two Tribunes – chuckled with appreciation. "... I am indeed, sir, a surgeon to old shoes; when they are in great danger, I re-cover them. As proper men as ever trod upon cowhide have walked upon my handiwork."

Flavius returned, "But why are you not in your shop today? Why do you lead these men about the streets?"

The cobbler answered, "Truly, sir, to wear out their shoes, to get myself into more work." The crowd regaled his wit with delight once more, then the bearded man decided to have mercy upon the flustered

Tribunes. "But indeed, sir, we make holiday to see *Caesar*, and to rejoice in his triumph."

The gathering cheered, but upon confirming that this obscene behavior truly had nothing to do with the Feast of Lupercal, the Tribunes stewed all the more.

In the Tribunes' eyes, this "triumph" of which the man spoke was cause for concern, not celebration. Julius Caesar's victory in Spain over the sons of Pompey – the former Triumvir along with Caesar himself and Crassus – was no great achievement for the Roman Republic, for it did not represent the defeat of any foreign adversaries, but those of *fellow Romans*. Why would this bring joy to any true Roman, this messy affair that reflected a dubious civil war more than an expansion of Rome's influence?

And these lowborn, hypocritical fools leaped upon this "triumph" as an excuse to abandon their shops and take to the streets!

Cutting through the lingering acclamations, Murellus vented, "Why 'rejoice'? What conquest does he bring home? What enslaved tributaries follow him to Rome, to grace his chariot wheels in captive bonds?"

The cobbler and carpenter and their fellow revelers looked at one another in uncertainty.

Murellus pressed on, voicing his disgust as he looked around and met each of their gazes. "You blocks, you stones, you worse than senseless things! Oh, you hard hearts, you cruel men of Rome, did you not know Pompey? Many times, and often, you have climbed up to walls and battlements, to towers and windows, yea, even to chimney tops, your infants in your arms, and have sat there the livelong day – with patient expectation – to see great Pompey pass the streets of Rome. And when you saw nothing but his chariot appear, have you not made such a universal shout that the river Tiber trembled underneath her banks to hear the echo of your sounds made in her concave shores?" He shook his head in disdain. "And do you now put on your best attire? And do you now cull out a 'holiday'? And do you now strew flowers in *his* way ..." He flung an arm toward the decorated bust of Caesar. "... who comes in 'triumph' over Pompey's offspring?"

The crowd had lost their celebratory vigor under this scathing rebuke, their eyes dropping to the street beneath their feet.

"Be gone!" he commanded. "Run to your houses, fall upon your knees, pray to the gods to defer the plague that must light upon this ingratitude."

On this street, at least, the cheery mood was quashed. The cobbler and all the rest shuffled about and away, their countenances draped in defeat and shame as they withdrew from the Tribunes.

Flavius called after them, "Go, go, good countrymen, and for this fault assemble all the poor men of your sort, draw them to Tiber's banks, and weep your tears into the channel, till the lowest streams do kiss the most exalted shores of all."

The retreating throng glanced back at him, then continued without any retort or comment.

With some satisfaction, Flavius said to Murellus, "See how even their basest natures are affected; they vanish tongue-tied in their guiltiness."

Murellus grunted, sharing his gratification that even the rowdiest of the lot were slinking away as silent as the rest.

Flavius then said, "You go down that way towards the Capitol, I will go this way." His lip curled in loathing as he again gazed upon the many petals that dressed the bust of Caesar, especially the one which rested crown-like upon the head. "Disrobe the images if you do find them decked with such ceremonial trappings."

Murellus nodded, but also expressed some concern; chastising the rabble for their excesses was one thing, but ... "May we do so? You know it *is* the Feast of Lupercal."

Flavius dismissed the notion with a wave of his hand. "It is no matter; let no images be hung with Caesar's trophies." With two strides, he approached the bust and ripped the crown-like wreath from its head. "I'll go about and drive away the vulgar commoners from the streets; you do so, too, where you perceive them too thick. These growing feathers *plucked* from Caesar's wing ..." He grabbed a handful of the wreaths from the bust's neck and tore them free with equal vehemence. "... will make him fly an *ordinary* falcon's flight, who would otherwise soar above the view of men and keep us all in servile fearfulness."

Murellus again grunted his agreement. These adulations from

the commoners for Caesar did not bode well. This was the Roman *Republic*, by the gods! The triumvirate of Pompey, Caesar, and Crassus had been too much power in too few hands as it was. But the pedestal upon which Caesar was now placed, this "dictator for life" they wished to honor him ... it was beyond the pale.

Shaking hands, the Tribunes of Rome parted ways.

PART ONE

CHAPTER TWO

Embracing with merry gusto the Feast of Lupercal, honored on the fifteenth of February, the crowds of proud, upper-class Romans surrounding the Capitol square elevated their celebration all the more for the presence of their beloved Julius Caesar. Trumpets flared, Roman centurions marched, commoners cast rose petals into the air and onto the streets of the square, all in praise of the Lupercalian rites, yes, but mostly in adoration of Caesar himself.

Behind the bannermen, trumpeters, and decorated soldiers, Caesar led the delegation, followed by Senators and Tribunes and other dignitaries, among them Casca, Marcus Brutus and his distant cousin Decius Brutus, Cicero, Caius Cassius [1], and of course, Caesar's wife, Calphurnia – Calphurnia, for her part, waved to the crowds while speaking in close tones with Portia, wife of Marcus Brutus. And behind the lot of them slunk Flavius and Murellus, both of whom cast nervous eyes toward the soldiers who seemed to be shadowing them.

As the procession neared the group of runners who stripped

---

[1]

Most historians believe that Caius Cassius' first name was, in fact, Gaius – his full given name "Gaius Cassius Longinus" – and yet, virtually all editions have Shakespeare naming him Caius, and the film and stage versions follow suit. It should be noted that "Gaius" was a very common first name in Ancient Rome, and "Caius" was an accepted variant spelling (an apparent reflection of early Roman confusion regarding the use of the Greek gamma – they used it for both the "g" and "k" sounds). Since Shakespeare chose to use this variant, I have kept him "Caius" in this work.

down in preparation for the ceremonial course through the heart of Rome, Caesar spied among them his good friend Mark Antony. Caesar smiled, halted his march, and called over his shoulder, "Calphurnia!"

Casca was quick to act, raising his hand and proclaiming to all around them, "Peace, ho! Caesar speaks."

Within seconds, the trumpeters ceased their music, and the commoners quieted their cheers.

"Calphurnia!" Caesar called for his wife again.

Calphurnia hurried from Portia's side to stand before her husband. "Here, my lord."

Caesar smiled. "You should stand directly in Antony's way when he does run his course." He turned toward the runners and summoned, "Antony!"

Like Calphurnia, Antony presented himself posthaste. "Caesar, my lord?"

Caesar placed a hand upon his friend's bare shoulder. "Do not forget in your speed, Antony, to touch Calphurnia." He smiled at his wife once more, though there was some slight condescension about it. "For our elders say the barren – when touched in this holy chase – shake off their sterile curse."

Calphurnia struggled to maintain a pleasant expression; many in Rome knew how much Caesar desired a biological heir to stand alongside his favored great-nephew, Octavius, and the burden fell to her (as his third wife, no less) to provide one – a burden which she had yet to fulfill. Still, she could not help but wish that Caesar had not made his request to Mark Antony so public.

For his part, Antony replied, "I shall remember. When Caesar says 'Do this,' it is performed."

This bold proclamation prompted several Senators and Tribunes to exchange wary glances – subtle glances, to be sure, yet they spoke volumes.

But Caesar nodded his approval, both at the promise and the praise. "Set on, and leave no ceremony out." He gave Antony an amiable shove, and Antony returned to the awaiting runners.

The festivities were warming once more, the procession getting back underway, when a harsh, piercing voice cried, *"Caesar!"*

Everyone hesitated, grumbling and looking around for the source of this terrible cry, one so unfitting for this time of celebration; many revelers were unnerved by its desperate timbre, and found themselves uncertain as to how to react.

Caesar himself appeared more intrigued than concerned. "Ha? Who calls?"

Casca again declared, "Bid every noise be still; peace, yet again!"

When the crowd fell closer to silence, Caesar asked, "Who is it in the pressing throng that calls on me? I heard a tongue shriller than all the music cry, 'Caesar!' " He offered an encouraging, benign smile. "Speak; Caesar is turned to hear."

The voice came again, weaker this time but still audible due to the lessened commotion of the crowd. "Beware the ides of March."

Caesar scanned the assembly. "What man is that?"

After a pregnant pause, it was Marcus Brutus who shouldered others aside, stood before someone too concealed for Caesar to see, then turned back and answered, "A soothsayer bids you 'beware the ides of March.' "

Caesar's brow furrowed; why should one such as he "beware" of the fifteenth of March? "Set him before me. Let me see his face."

Cassius stepped forward from his cluster of Senators to call, "Fellow, come from the throng; look upon Caesar."

Near Brutus, the crowd parted. A decrepit figure limped forward; his visage made one shudder at its heavy decay, like a man who had partaken of far too much wine and ended up with one foot already in the grave. He peered at Caesar with his single good eye, the other drifting too high and outward.

And in that eye, Caesar thought he saw something like adoration and devotion; he did not recoil from the unseemly fellow, but asked, "What do you say to me now? Speak once again."

When the dilapidated man responded, his voice was so strained and creaky, it was a wonder his initial cries had penetrated the ovations. With earnest sincerity, he rasped to Caesar, "Beware the ides of March."

Caesar met that gentle eye and pondered this warning ... but, in the end, he took on a kind yet patronizing smile and declared for those around him, "He is a dreamer. Let us leave him." He then raised his hand high and waved the procession onward. "Pass!"

The soothsayer reached out to Caesar, as though to touch his robes and implore him to listen further, but the looming presence of the nearest soldiers dissuaded him; the dilapidated man sagged, and even as the trumpets sounded once more and the cortège continued along its way, he disappeared back into the crowd.

But it was not only the soothsayer who broke away from the delegation. Cassius stepped back, allowing others to pass him as he maintained a fixed, neutral expression. For he had noticed Brutus – brother to Cassius' wife, Junia – making his own way apart from the celebrations and along a relatively quiet street. Cassius hesitated only a brief moment before pursuing his brother-in-law.

As they left the greatest din behind them, Cassius called to Brutus, "Will you go see the order of the race's course?"

Brutus glanced over his shoulder in mild surprise at having been addressed. He shook his head and replied, "Not I."

Cassius offered a meager gesture back the way from which they had come. "I pray you, do."

Brutus smiled and shook his head again. "I am not gamesome. I do lack some part of that lively spirit that is in Mark Antony." He echoed Cassius' own gesture toward the center of celebration. "Do not let me hinder your desires, Cassius. I'll leave you." He continued along his way.

Cassius blinked at the rather abrupt dismissal. But he paused a mere handful of heartbeats before hurrying after him. "Brutus ..."

Brutus halted again and turned back, his expression mild but expectant.

Cassius considered his words before speaking, "I have observed you of late. I have not seen, from your eyes, that same gentleness and show of love as I was wont to have." He placed his hand upon his own chest. "You bear too stubborn and too strange a hand over your friend who loves you."

Brutus winced at this revelation, then offered another, gentler smile of warmth. "Cassius, do not be misled. If I have veiled my expression, I turn the trouble of my countenance merely upon *myself*. I am vexed of late with conflicted passions – conceptions only relating *to* myself, which give some stain, perhaps, to my behaviors." He offered Cassius a light touch upon his shoulder. "But therefore do not let my good friends be grieved – among which number, Cassius, you be one – nor construe any further my neglect than that poor Brutus, at war with himself, forgets the shows of love to other men."

A third time Brutus attempted to continue on his way, away from the revelries behind them, but this time Cassius did not allow him to take more than a single step before trailing after him. "Then, Brutus, I have much mistook your passion, because of which this breast of mine has buried thoughts of great value, worthy cogitations." He hurried several long strides so that he could halt in front of Brutus and ask, "Tell me, good Brutus, can you see your face?"

Brutus paused, cocking his head to one side. "No, Cassius, for the eye sees not *itself*, except by reflection from other things."

A shrewd expression crossed Cassius' face as he nodded. "It is true. And it is very much lamented, Brutus, that you have no such mirrors as will turn your hidden *worthiness* into your eye, that you might see your reflection." When Brutus offered no response beyond a raised eyebrow, Cassius pressed onward. "I have heard where many of those with the best standing in Rome ... the best, except for immortal Caesar ... speaking of Brutus, and groaning underneath this era's yoke, have wished that noble Brutus had his eyes."

Brutus regarded Cassius with his own acumen, and, in spite of the continuing commotions of revelry behind them, lowered his voice. "Into what dangers would you lead me, Cassius, that you would have me seek into myself for that which is not *in* me?"

"As to that, good Brutus," Cassius retorted, "be prepared to hear. And since you know you cannot see yourself so well as by reflection ... *I*, your looking glass, will modestly discover to yourself that *of* yourself which you yet know not of." He held up a forestalling hand as Brutus made to protest. "And do not be suspicious of me, gentle Brutus: Were I a common jester, or did cheapen my love with frequent oaths to every new professor of friendship; if you know that I do fawn on men and hug them hard, then afterward defame them; or if you know that I profess friendship in drunken banqueting to all the mob ... *then* consider me dangerous."

Brutus opened his mouth to respond, but at that moment, the trumpeters from the festival's procession loosed their loudest song yet. And though the delegation had left them far behind, neither Brutus nor Cassius could dismiss the exultant shouting of the distant crowds that followed an instant later.

Even as the echoes lingered, Brutus shook his head and said, almost to himself, "What does this shouting mean? I do fear the people choose Caesar for their *king*."

Cassius studied him. "Aye, do you fear it? Then I must think you would not have it so."

"I would *not*, Cassius ... yet I love him well." Brutus heaved a wearisome sigh; then he snapped his attention back to Cassius – who still stood in his way – demanding, "But why do you hold me here so long? What is it that you would impart to me?" When Cassius held his ground, yet appeared hesitant to speak further, Brutus assured him, "If it be, in any respect, toward the general good, then set honor in one eye and death in the other, and I will look on both impartially – for let the gods so favor me, as I love the name of honor more than I fear death."

Cassius, looking pleased, nodded at this. Clasping his hands to the front of his robes, he said, "I know that virtue to be in you, Brutus, as well as I do know your outward appearance. Well, honor *is* the subject of my story ..."

As he spoke, Cassius drifted toward a nearby marble bench which waited upon this quiet street for citizens to settle and rest as desired. He gestured for Brutus to join him.

"I cannot tell what you and other men think of this life," Cassius continued, "but, for my single self, I desire not to live in awe of such a thing as common as I myself. I was born as free as Caesar, and so were you; we both have fed as well, and we can both endure the winter's cold as well as he.

"For once, upon a raw and gusty day, the troubled river Tiber chafing against her shores, Caesar said to me, 'Do you dare, Cassius, now leap with me into this angry flood and swim to yonder point?' Upon the word, clothed as I was, I plunged in and bade him follow; so indeed, he did. The torrent roared, and we did buffet it with lusty sinews, throwing it aside and stemming it with hearts of competition. But before we could arrive at the proposed point, Caesar cried, 'Help me, Cassius, or I sink!' And I – as Aeneas, our great ancestor, did bear upon his shoulder his father, the old Anchises, from the flames of Troy – so from the waves of Tiber I did bear the tired Caesar." Cassius shook his head in disgust, and scoffed in a lower voice, "And *this* man has now become a god, and Cassius is a wretched creature and must bend his body if Caesar carelessly nods to him."

Cassius paused as another heightened cry echoed through the streets of Rome. He and Brutus exchanged an anxious look as the uproar peaked, then fell. When finally the noise returned to the general hubbub of city life, Cassius continued.

"Caesar had a fever when he was in Spain," he shared (in a taletelling tone that did not sit altogether well with Brutus), "and when the fit was on him, I did mark how he did shake – it is true, this 'god' did shake. His lips fled their healthy hue as cowardly soldiers might fly from the color of their own flags, and that same eye ... whose glance *awes* the world ... did lose its luster. I did hear him groan. Aye, and that tongue of his that bade the Romans mark him and write his speeches in their books, 'Alas!' it cried, as a sick girl, 'give me some drink, Titinius!'"

This time, Cassius shook his head with such vehemence, Brutus would not have been surprised if he had spat upon the ground.

"You gods," Cassius growled with a glance flicked toward the heavens, "it does amaze me that a man of such a feeble constitution should so outstrip the majestic world, and bear the palm of victory *alone*."

The two men perked up as the city echoed yet again with cries of rabble joy, followed by another flourish of trumpets.

"Another general shout!" Brutus proclaimed, his brow furrowing. "I do believe that these applauses are for some new honors that are heaped on Caesar."

Cassius sneered, "Why, man, he does bestride the narrow world – like the giant Colossus did bestride the harbor of Greece's Rhodes – and *we* petty men walk under his huge legs and peep about to find ourselves dishonorable graves. Men at some time are masters of their fates." He stood, as though to walk away, but instead locked eyes with Brutus. "The fault, dear Brutus, is not in our stars, but in *ourselves*, that we are underlings. 'Brutus' and 'Caesar': What should be in that name, 'Caesar'? Why should that name be voiced more than yours? Write them together, yours is as fair a name; speak them, it does flatter the mouth as well; weigh them, it is as heavy; conjure with them, 'Brutus' will raise a spirit as soon as 'Caesar.'"

This time Cassius did walk away, but it was only to begin pacing to and fro, casting his eye in the direction of the repeated shouts and flourishes, and it was clear that the man struggled to keep his voice level in his acrimony.

"Now," he continued, "in the names of all the gods at once, upon what meat does this – our Caesar – feed that he is grown so great? Era, you are shamed! Rome, you have lost the breeding of noble bloods! When was there ever an age – since the great flood of Deucalion – that was famous for no more than with *one* man? When could they who talked of Rome say – till now – that her wide walks encompassed but *one* man? Now is it Rome indeed ... and room enough ... when there is in it but only *one* man."

Brutus noted that Cassius had stressed the similar pronunciation between "Rome" and "room" here, merging them into a spiteful play on words. Before he could give it further thought, Cassius whirled and returned to the bench, again piercing Brutus with his passionate gaze.

"Oh," he continued, "you and I have heard our fathers say there was a Brutus once – Lucius Junius Brutus, your very ancestor who expelled the Tarquins to establish our great Republic – who would have tolerated the eternal *devil* to keep his throne in Rome ..." He sneered toward the departed procession once more. "... as easily as a *king*."

Cassius appeared to have finally lost his momentum, and Brutus drew a long, deliberate breath, considering his words with care before responding.

"That you do love me," he told Cassius, "I am not at all doubtful. What you would *work me* to ... I have some idea. How I have thought of this – and of these times – I shall recount hereafter."

Cassius leaned forward, making as though to speak further, but

Brutus forestalled him with a gentle but firm hand.

"For this present," he continued, "I would not be any further persuaded– so, with love, I ask you to halt. What you have said I will consider; what you have yet to say I will, with patience, hear, and find a proper time both to hear and to answer such high things. Till then, my noble friend, chew upon this ..." It was his turn to lock eyes with his companion, and to fill his words with heartfelt intensity. "Brutus would rather be a common villager than to repute himself a son of Rome under these hard conditions, as this time is likely to lay upon us."

Something flickered in Cassius' face, in his eyes – something quick, and perhaps furtive. Then his countenance relaxed, and he appeared both pleased and relieved. "I am glad that my weak words have struck at least this much show of fire from Brutus."

Yet another commotion arose throughout the city, but this one lingered, the calls and trumpets yielding to extended applause. Soon, the rumblings pulled into focus, concentrating more toward the main thoroughfare from which the two men had come.

Brutus swallowed a sigh. "The games are done, and Caesar is returning." With a gesture for Cassius to follow, he stood from the bench and led the way back toward the source of their shared angst. It soon grew clear that the throng of commoners were forming a virtual wall through which they would not easily pass, even with their robes of office. Instead, Brutus guided Cassius to one side, so that they might climb a high stoop before a closed shop. From there, they could observe, over the heads of the fawning citizens, the approaching Caesar and his servile retinue; the soldiers cleared a path before their *Dictator Perpetuo*, keeping the citizens' outstretched hands at bay and leaving the way all the more visible.

Cassius leaned closer to Brutus' ear and murmured, "As they pass by, pluck Casca by the sleeve, and he will – after his sour fashion – tell you what has proceeded worthy of note today."

Brutus nodded in distracted fashion. "I will do so. But look you, Cassius ..." He inclined his head toward the approaching Caesar, who, Brutus observed, scowled as he leaned his left arm on the shoulder of a sweaty, downtrodden Antony. "The angry spot does glow on Caesar's brow, and all the rest look like a scolded train –

Calphurnia's cheek is pale, and Cicero looks with such ferret-like and fiery eyes as we have seen him in the Capitol, being crossed in debate by some Senators."

Cassius nodded his agreement and repeated with confidence, "Casca will tell us what the matter is." And, leading Brutus from the stoop, they descended and shouldered their way into the crowd, attempting to intercept Casca before he passed by ...

Caesar, preoccupied though he might have been, noticed Cassius' movements, and inclined his head toward his younger friend. "Antony!" he snapped.

Antony straightened. "Caesar."

Caesar regarded him, and his expression softened as he spoke for Antony's ears only. "Let me have men about me who are fat; smooth-foreheaded men and such as sleep at night." He raised his eyebrows in a particular direction; Antony glanced with subtlety to spy who Caesar was indicating. "Yonder Cassius has a lean and hungry look. He thinks too much. Such men are dangerous."

Antony dismissed the Senator, who shuffled through the crowd. "Do not fear him, Caesar; he's not dangerous. He is a noble Roman, and well disposed."

Caesar grumbled, "I wish he were fatter! But I do not fear him. Yet ... if I *were* liable to fear, I do not know the man I should avoid so soon as that spare Cassius. He reads much, he is a great observer, and he looks right through the deeds of men. He loves no plays, as you do, Antony; he hears no music; seldom he smiles – and then he smiles in such a sort as if he mocked himself, and scorned his spirit that could be moved to smile at anything." Caesar grunted in distaste. "Such men as he are never at heart's ease while they behold a greater personage than themselves, and therefore they are very dangerous. I rather tell you what is to *be* feared than what *I* fear; for always *I* am Caesar." Then he offered Antony a warm smile. "Come on my right hand, for this ear is deaf, and tell me – truly – what you think of him."

And, as Antony switched from Caesar's left side to his right, the trumpets played on and the retinue continued along its way. All save Casca, who lingered behind when he felt Brutus' hand upon him ...

As Brutus extracted Casca from the procession, Casca observed with some wry amusement, "You pulled me by the cloak. Would you speak with me?"

"Aye, Casca," Brutus answered him, "tell us what has occurred today that Caesar looks so serious."

Casca raised an eyebrow. "Why, you were with him, were you not?"

Brutus raised his own eyebrow and smiled in return. "Then I should not ask Casca what had occurred."

Casca chuckled and nodded his acceptance of this fair point. Then he explained, "Why, there was a *crown* offered to Caesar; and, being offered to him, he put it by with the back of his hand, thus ..." Casca pantomimed brushing something away, like a citizen declining an unsavory goblet of wine. "... and then the people fell a-shouting."

Brutus noted that Casca said "people" with distaste. "What was the second noise for?"

Casca shrugged, repeating a half-hearted encore of his brushing-away gesture. "Why, for that, too."

Cassius spoke, "They shouted thrice. What was the last cry for?"

Casca shrugged again. "Why, for that, too."

Brutus clarified, "Was the crown offered him *thrice*?"

Casca nodded, his expression sour. "Aye, indeed it was, and he put it by thrice, every time gentler than the other; and at every putting-by, my honest neighbors shouted."

Cassius demanded, "Who offered him the crown?"

"Why," Casca said, as though the answer should be obvious, "Antony."

Cassius tensed, his jaws clenching in antipathy, but Brutus placed a calming hand upon his arm and said, "Tell us the manner of it, noble Casca."

Casca waved his hand and scoffed, "I can as well be hanged as tell the 'manner' of it. It was mere foolery; I did not mark it." But when he saw that neither Brutus nor Cassius were going to let him dismiss them so easily, he acquiesced. "I saw Mark Antony offer Caesar a crown – yet it was not a crown, neither; it was one of these garland coronets of a Lupercal runner – and, as I told you, Caesar put it by once; but for all that, to my thinking, he would willingly have had it. Then Antony offered it to him again; then he put it by again; but, to my thinking, he was very loath to lay his fingers off it. And then Antony offered it the third time; he put it the third time by; and each time as he refused it ..." Casca's faced contracted in disgust. "...the rabblement hooted and clapped their chapped hands, and threw up their sweaty nightcaps, and uttered such a deal of stinking breath because Caesar refused the crown that it had almost *choked* Caesar, for he fainted and fell down at it." His sickened lips puckered further. "And for my own part, I dared not laugh for fear of opening *my* lips and receiving the bad air."

Casca expected his disdainful commentary on the commoners to invoke humor from his audience of two, but Cassius fixated elsewhere. "But wait, I pray you: What, did Caesar *faint*?"

Casca nodded. "He fell down in the marketplace and foamed at the mouth and was speechless."

Brutus offered his own knowing nod. "It is very likely; he has the 'falling sickness' – epilepsy."

Cassius scowled, again appearing as though he desired to spit upon the ground. "No, Caesar does not have it. But you and I and honest Casca, *we* have the *falling* sickness."

Casca, having missed Cassius' earlier diatribe against Caesar's rise to power, said only, "I do not know what you mean by that, but I am sure Caesar fell down. If the common people did not clap him and hiss him, accordingly as he pleased and *dis*pleased them – as they used to do the actors in the theatre – then I am no honest man."

Brutus asked, "What did he say when he came to himself?"

Casca elaborated, "Indeed, before he fell down, when he perceived the common herd was glad he refused the crown, he plucked open his doublet and offered them his throat to cut." He smirked as he recalled the absurdity of it. "If *I* had been a working man of any occupation, if I would not have taken him at his word ... I imagine I might go to hell among the rogues." He shrugged. "And so he fell. When he came to himself again, he said, if he had done or said anything amiss, he desired their worships to think it was his infirmity. Three or four wenches, where I stood, cried, 'Alas, good soul!' and forgave him with all their hearts." He sneered, "But there's no heed to be taken of *them*; if Caesar had stabbed their mothers, they would have done no less."

"And after that," Brutus clarified, "he came away, looking

serious?"

"Aye."

Recalling their fellow statesman's fiery eyes, Cassius asked, "Did Cicero say anything?"

"Aye, he spoke Greek."

"To what effect?"

Casca smirked. "Nay, if I tell you that, I'll never look you in the face again. Those that understood him smiled at one another and shook their heads; but for *my* own part ..." His smirk broadened into a smile. "... it was Greek to me."

Again, neither Brutus nor Cassius were in the mood to receive his humor. Upon seeing this, Casca grew serious once more. He leaned in toward the men, speaking lower than he had before.

"I could tell you more news, too," he told them. "Murellus and Flavius – for pulling decorations off Caesar's statues – have been put to silence."

Brutus and Cassius locked eyes. Two Tribunes of Rome, punished with dismissal over such a minor discourtesy! It stood as a solid example of every concern they had discussed this day.

Having nothing else to share, Casca stepped back and said to both, "Fare you well. There was more foolery yet, if I could remember it."

Cassius nodded in shared abhorrence. He then asked, "Will you have supper with me tonight, Casca?"

"No," Casca stated, "I have a prior engagement."

Cassius tried again, "Will you dine with me tomorrow?"

Casca thought about it. "Aye, if I am alive, and your mind solid, and your dinner worth the eating."

Brutus thought this a rather rude reply to Cassius' kind invitation, yet Cassius appeared to think little of it. "Good. I will expect you."

"Do so," Casca said, then offered a short wave. "Farewell, both." And then the man was on his way.

Brutus shook his head and commented, "What a blunt fellow this man has grown to be! He was high-spirited when he went to school."

Cassius retorted, "So is he now in execution of any bold or

noble enterprise, notwithstanding that he puts on this sluggish form. This rudeness is a sauce to his good wit, which gives men stomach to digest his words with better appetite."

Brutus wasn't sure of all that, but he had no desire to debate the matter, so he simply said, "And so it is." He then took a step away to follow after Casca's example. "For this time, I will leave you. Tomorrow – if you please to speak with me – I will come to your home; or, if you prefer, come to my home, and I will wait for you."

"I will do so. Till then, think of the state of the world."

Brutus nodded and went on his way ... and Cassius stared after him.

Well, Brutus, you are noble. Yet I see your honorable mettle may be molded from that to which it is disposed – therefore, it is appropriate that 'noble' minds keep ever with those like-minded; for who is so firm that they cannot be seduced?

Caesar does bear a grudge against me, but he loves *Brutus. If I were Brutus now and he were Cassius, Brutus would not persuade me.*

This night I will throw writings in his windows – in several handwritings, as if they came from several citizens – all sharing the great opinion that Rome holds of his name; wherein, obscurely, Caesar's ambition shall be glanced at. And after this ...

Let Caesar seat himself sure, for we will shake *him ... or worse days shall endure.*

PART ONE

CHAPTER THREE

Thunder and lightning and wind, and more – too much more, the likes of which were wicked strangers to noble Rome.

Nearly one month had passed since the Feast of Lupercal, and times had fallen dark indeed. Now the ides of March loomed on the morrow, and the Senate was due to meet with Caesar on some urgent matter ... but on this foul night, Casca could not imagine any civilized Romans leaving the safety of their homes tomorrow if conditions did not change, and swiftly.

Oh, there were rumors abound as to the purpose of the Senatorial summons: Word came that Caesar planned to march into the east with his great Roman forces, to make war upon the Parthians – nearly a decade ago, the Parthians destroyed good Crassus and most of his army, and many declared that this defeat had gone too long unredressed.

Some said that Caesar sought a formal declaration of war from the Senate; others suggested that perhaps he wanted to establish a sort of regency, to govern Rome in his absence.

And others still believed it had nothing at all to do with the Parthians. That Caesar's sole objective was to secure his long-expected crown, once and for all.

Another bolt of lightning lit the night sky, and Casca cringed, his hand tightening on the hilt of his drawn short-sword. The thunder which followed on its heels shook his very bones. He paused, waiting for more to fall from the heavens – more *fire*, perchance? – but for the moment, all that assailed him was the malicious wind.

Why was he out on such a night as this, sword in hand? Was he losing his mind? A summons to meet with good Cassius was not enough! He should turn back, go home, give himself conditions under which he might ponder the meaning of all—

A shadowy figure appeared on the street before him. Casca gasped, hefting his sword higher ...

"Good evening, Casca," came Cicero's calm, unconcerned voice, raised only enough to be heard over the howling wind. "Did you escort Caesar home?"

Casca forced himself to relax – or rather, he attempted to do so – and lowered his gladius blade.

Cicero gawked at him. "Why are you breathless?" he asked Casca with concern. "And why do you stare so?"

The man's aplomb struck Casca speechless at first. Finally, he retorted, "Are *you* not moved, when all the rule of Earth shakes like a thing unfirm?" He shuddered. "Oh, Cicero, I have seen tempests when the scolding winds have split the knotty oaks, and I have seen the ambitious ocean swell, and rage, and foam, to be exalted with the threatening clouds ... but never till tonight, never till now, did I go through a tempest dropping *fire*." He shook his head, his eyes wide as he peered up at the starless sky. "Either there is a civil strife in heaven, or else the world, too insolent with the gods, incenses them to send destruction."

Cicero's expression – what Casca could see of it in this cursed darkness, with so few street torches standing against the wind – remained placid, unmoved by Casca's fear. "Why, did you see anything extraordinarily wondrous?"

Determined to shake the man as he was shaken, Casca told him, "A common slave – you know him well by sight – held up his left hand, which did flame and burn like twenty torches joined; and yet his hand, not sensitive to the fire, remained unscorched. Besides that – I have not since put away my sword! – against the Capitol I met a *lion*, who gazed upon me and went surly by, without harming me. And there were, huddled close together, a hundred pale women, transformed with their fear, who swore they saw men – *all* in fire – walking up and down the streets." Then another thought struck him. "And yesterday, a screech-owl, the bird of night, sat upon the marketplace even at noonday, hooting and shrieking." He shook his head in disbelief even as his hands trembled. "When these amazing prodigies meet so conjointly, do not let men say, 'These things have their reasons, they are natural,' for *I* believe they are *portentous* things unto the region that they point toward."

Still Cicero appeared unmoved, and he even offered Casca a patronizing smile as he said, "Indeed, it is a strangely-disposed time. But men may construe things after their fashion, contrary to the 'purpose' of the things themselves." And with that, he seemed to consider the matter closed. "Does Caesar come to the Capitol tomorrow?"

Casca, caught by the abrupt change of subject, could only answer, "He does; for he did bid Antony send word to you that he would be there tomorrow."

Cicero nodded. "Goodnight then, Casca. This disturbed weather is not fit to walk in." And with that, he strode off.

Casca called after him, "Farewell, Cicero." As condescending as the man had been, Casca found himself wanting for the company on this night.

"Who's there?"

Casca nearly cried out at the sudden voice that called from the darkness behind him. Brandishing his gladius sword once again, he blurted, "A Roman."

"Casca, by your voice."

Casca relaxed, his shoulders slumping and his blade pointing to the street in stark relief. "Your ear is good. Cassius, what a night is this!"

Cassius emerged from the shadows and joined him. "A very pleasing night to *honest* men."

Aghast, Casca could not have disagreed more. "Whoever knew the heavens could menace so?"

"Those that have known the Earth so full of faults!" Cassius snapped, his vehemence jolting Casca from some of his fear. "For my part," Cassius continued with fierce pride, "I have walked about the streets, submitting myself to the perilous night; and so – with my doublet unfastened, Casca, as you see – I have bared my bosom to the elements; and when the bent blue lightning seemed to open the breast of heaven, I did present myself even in the aim and very flash of it."

Casca remained taken aback. "But *why* did you so much tempt the heavens? It is the role of men to fear and tremble when the most mighty gods, by tokens, send such dreadful heralds to astonish us."

Cassius glowered at Casca with such disappointment, even the gloom could not mask it. "You are dull, Casca, and you do lack – or else you do not use – those sparks of life that should be in a Roman. You look pale, and gaze, and display fear, and give yourself to awe, to see the strange impatience of the heavens." Cassius gripped him by the shoulders, his fingers clenched enough to bring Casca discomfort. "But if you would consider the *true* cause: *Why* all these fires, *why* all these gliding ghosts, *why* birds and beasts stray from their natural character, *why* old men, fools, and children prophesize, why *all these things* change from their order, their natures, and innate faculties, to aberrant quality ... why, then you shall find that heaven has infused them with these spirits, to make them instruments of fear and *warning* to some unnatural commonwealth." With that, Cassius released his shoulders, yet held Casca captive with his ferocious eyes. "Now I could, Casca, name to you a man most like this dreadful night, who thunders, lightenings, opens graves, and roars as does a lion in the Capitol – a man no mightier than yourself or me in personal action, yet has grown as prodigious, and as frightful, as these strange eruptions are."

Casca swallowed, his dry throat clicking. "It is *Caesar* that you mean, is it not, Cassius?"

"Let it be who it is." Cassius' words were dismissive, yet his delivery was anything but. "For Romans now have sinews and limbs like their ancestors; but, woe to this age, our fathers' minds are dead, and we are governed with our mothers' spirits; our tolerance of our yoke shows us womanish."

Casca nodded, both in agreement and to placate his friend's temper. "Indeed, they say the Senators mean to establish Caesar as a *king* tomorrow, and he shall wear his crown by sea and land – in every place, save here in Italy."

Cassius sneered, reached beneath his cloak, jerked free a dagger with such flourish that Casca flinched back ... until Cassius held the blade close to his own throat. "I know where I will wear this dagger, then; Cassius, from bondage, will deliver Cassius." He scrutinized the dark, stormy sky. "In this, you gods, you make the weak most strong;

in this, you gods, you do defeat tyrants. Neither stony tower, nor walls of beaten brass, nor airless dungeon, nor strong links of iron, can retain the strength of a spirit ... but *life*, being weary of these worldly bars, never lacks power to dismiss itself." He turned back to Casca, his dagger still held aloft but no longer aimed at himself. "If I know this, know all the world besides, that part of tyranny that I do bear I can shake off at my pleasure."

Thunder rumbled over the city, but for the first time, it did not make Casca cower. Instead, he hefted his sword once more and replied to Cassius, "So can I. So *every* bondman bears, in his own hand, the power to cancel his captivity."

"And why," Cassius demanded, "should Caesar be a tyrant, then? Poor man! I know he would not be a wolf, except that he sees the Romans are nothing but sheep; he would not be a lion, if Romans were not like the red doe. Those who, with haste, will make a mighty fire begin it with weak straws." He shook his head in anger, and in revulsion. "What trash is Rome, what rubbish, and what offal, when it serves for the base matter to illuminate so vile a thing as *Caesar*!"

Cassius stared at the dagger in his hand, then shifted his gaze to Casca as if just recalling that he was present.

"But, oh grief," he spoke in a lower voice, "where have you led me? I, perhaps, speak this before a *willing* bondman; then, I know I must be made to answer for my words." He gripped his dagger tighter. "But I am armed, and dangers are indifferent to me."

Casca shook his head. "You speak to Casca," he assured his friend, "and to such a man who is no mocking telltale." When Cassius parted his lips to respond, Casca cut him off, "Hold, take my hand."

Cassius remained silent as Casca seized his hand within his own.

"Be active for redress of all these grievances," Casca proclaimed, "and I will set this foot of mine as far as whoever goes farthest."

Cassius shook the hand holding his. "*There's* a bargain made." And when he released his grip, he smiled. "Now you should know, Casca, I have already moved some certain of the noblest-minded Romans to undertake with me an enterprise of honorable-dangerous consequence. And I do know, by this time, they wait for me in

Pompey's Porch."

Casca nodded; he knew well the magnificent portico of the theatre built by the great Pompey.

Cassius continued, "For now, this fearful night, there is no one stirring or walking in the streets ..." He glanced heavenward. "... and the complexion of the sky is like the work we have in hand: Most bloody, fiery, and most *terrible*."

Casca offered his own smile, but it dropped away when he caught movement from the corner of his eye. Taking Cassius by the arm, he attempted to draw his friend further into the shadows. "Stand back awhile, for here comes someone in haste."

But Cassius pulled free and patted his shoulder. "It is Cinna; I do know him by his gait. He is a friend." As the figure drew nearer, Cassius called out, "Cinna, where do you hurry so?"

"To find you," the newcomer replied. Then he stopped short. "Who's that? Metellus Cimber?"

Cassius shook his head and patted his companion upon the shoulder again. "No, it is Casca, one affiliated with our attempts." Then he cocked his head. "Am I not waited for, Cinna?"

But Cinna was still looking at Casca as he joined them and said, "I am glad of it." Then he peered up into the storming sky and drew his cloak tighter around him. "What a fearful night this is! There's two or three of us who have seen strange sights."

"Am I not waited for?" Cassius repeated with some impatience. "Tell me."

Cinna snapped free of his distraction. "Yes, you are. Oh, Cassius, if you could but win the noble Marcus Brutus to our party—"

Cassius cut him off. "Be content." He reached within his own cloak, drawing forth three small scrolls; as he instructed Cinna, he placed each in turn into the man's hand. "Good Cinna, take this paper, and be sure you lay it in the magistrate's chair, where only Brutus may find it ... and throw this in at his window ... set this up, with wax, upon old Brutus' statue. When all this is done, return to Pompey's Porch, where you shall find us. Are Decius Brutus and Trebonius there?"

Cinna tucked the scrolls away as he answered, "All but Metellus Cimber, and he's gone to seek you at your house." He bowed and stepped away. "Well, I will hurry and so bestow these papers as you bade me."

Cassius reiterated, "That done, return to Pompey's Theater."

Cinna nodded and hastened across the dark, windswept street.

Satisfied, Cassius said to his companion, "Come, Casca, you and I will yet, before daylight, see Brutus at his house." He grinned in knowing fashion. "Three parts of him is ours already, and the entire man – upon the next encounter – yields himself ours."

Casca sighed his relief. "Oh, he sits high in all the people's hearts; and that which would appear offensive in us, *his* support – like richest alchemy – will change to virtue and to worthiness."

Cassius agreed, "Him and his worth – and our great need of him – you have right well understood. Let us go, for it is after midnight, and before day we will awake him and be *sure* of him."

The men nodded to one another, then launched themselves into the stormy night.

PART TWO

CHAPTER ONE

Thunder continued its rumbling browbeating of Rome. Yet Marcus Brutus believed that its tyrannical grip was loosening, the lightning which ushered it striking further away, the great winds dying by inches, and the intense meteor shower – though still very bright in the dark sky – insinuated less threat than before. As he stood and surveyed the casual devastation the fierce weather had wrought upon his orchard, he gauged this thunder and those falling stars to be little more than an epilogue to this dreadful night.

But Brutus had not required these ghastly elements to lose sleep. Indeed, he had slept so few nights since his critical, and perilous, conversations with Cassius had begun ...

Peering about the darkness of his ravaged orchard, he called over his shoulder to his servant, "What, Lucius, ho!" As he waited, he looked to the sky again, but the ominous clouds remained too thick, punctured by the inexorable meteor shower more than the firmament above. He murmured, "I cannot, by the progress of the stars, give guess as to how near it is to day ..."

Indeed, it was late – or early, as it were – but he felt mild surprise that Lucius had not yet presented himself. He called again, "Lucius, I say!" When the boy still did not appear, he could not help but smile in admitted envy. *I wish it were* my *flaw, to sleep so soundly.*

Still, if one were to maintain a solid hold on one's own manor, it would not be prudent to indulge such a lackluster response.

Raising his voice – but not too loud, so as to avoid awakening his wife, Portia – he called yet again, "When, Lucius, *when*? Awake, I say! What, Lucius!"

At last, young Lucius stumbled out into the orchard, still rubbing the sleep from his eyes with one hand. "You called, my lord?"

"Get me a taper in my study, Lucius," Brutus instructed. "When it is lighted, come here and call me."

Lucius bowed as he backed away. "I will, my lord." He then hurried off to light the candle as his lord commanded.

Thunder rolled over Rome once more, and this heaven's rumble reflected Brutus' disposition.

It must *be by Caesar's death,* Brutus concluded, and not for the first time these past days and weeks. *And, for my part, I know no personal cause to strike at him, except for the general good. He desires to be crowned: How that might change his nature, there's the question – it is the bright day that brings forth the snake, and that demands wary walking. Crown him king, and then, I grant, we put a stinger in him that, at his will, he may do danger with.*

The abuse of "greatness" is when it disjoins compassion *from power; and, to speak truth of Caesar, I have not known when his passions swayed him more than his reason. But it is a common, proven experience that false humility is young ambition's ladder, to which the upward-climber turns his face ... but, once he attains the upmost round, he then, onto the ladder, turns his back, looks in the clouds, scorning the base rungs by which he did ascend.*

So Caesar may; then, for fear that he may, we prevent. *And since the attack will bear no justification for the thing he currently is, we must present it this way: That what he is, augmented, would run to these and these* extremes.

And therefore ... think of Caesar as a serpent's egg *– which, when hatched, would, as is his nature, grow mischievous – and* kill *him in the shell.*

A footfall from behind lured Brutus from his dark reverie. He turned to find Lucius approaching him with a small scroll in his hand.

"The taper burns in your study, sir," the boy reported. His features then tightened into a mask of endearing befuddlement as he proffered the scroll to his master. "Searching the window for a flint, I found this paper, thus sealed up, and I am sure it did not lie there when I went to bed."

Brutus accepted the scroll, which he suspected would be like the others he had discovered here and about over the past weeks. Nodding his thanks, he told the boy, with a kind smile, "Get you to bed again. It is not day."

Bowing his weary gratitude, Lucius turned away to do just that.

But at the last moment, still looking down upon this latest scroll, a memory struck Brutus. He asked, "Is not tomorrow, boy, the ides of March?"

Lucius thought for a moment, then admitted, "I do not know, sir."

Brutus was not, as a rule, given to superstition, but of late the words of that soothsayer on the Feast of Lupercal weighed upon his conflicted mind. "Look in the calendar," he instructed, "and bring me word."

"I will, sir," Lucius nodded, and scampered off.

Brutus contemplated the scroll in his hand. Though the gloom endured throughout his orchard, the meteor shower offered abiding pulses of light. *The falling stars,* he realized, *whizzing in the air, give so much light that I may read by them.*

Breaking the seal, he unrolled the scroll and read under his breath:

"'Brutus, you sleep. Awake, and see yourself! Shall Rome, et cetera ... Speak, strike, redress! Brutus, you sleep; awake!'"

He considered this, and all the other notes he had found. *Such instigations have been often dropped where I have took them up.* He regarded the scroll. *"Shall Rome, Et cetera." Thus I must piece it out: Shall Rome stand under one man's awe? What,* Rome? *My ancestors did drive the Tarquin from the streets of Rome when* he *was called a king.* He looked upon the scroll again. *"Speak, strike, redress!" Am I entreated to speak and strike?*

Oh, Rome, I make you this promise: If the redress will follow, you shall receive your full measure at the hand of Brutus.

As Brutus contemplated this private oath and the commitment thereof, Lucius returned to the orchard. "Sir, March has passed fourteen days." [2]

Brutus absorbed this confirmation, mulled over it: The ides of March was upon them. Again, he did not consider himself a superstitious man ... and yet, the *timing* of it ...

A knock echoed through the manor, startling the boy at this hour but failing to amaze Brutus at all.

"It is good," Brutus said, ostensibly to the information the boy had just imparted, but carrying a greater meaning beyond. "Go to the gate; somebody knocks."

Lucius bowed, then hurried off to obey.

Since Cassius did first whet me against Caesar, Brutus thought, *I have not slept well. Between the acting of a dreadful thing and the first instigation, all the interim is like a vision, or a hideous dream. The spirit and the body are then in council, and the state of man – like a little kingdom – suffers then the unsettled nature of an insurrection.*

Lucius reappeared, looking ever more as though he wanted nothing else but to return to bed.

"Sir," the boy reported, "it is your brother-in-law, Cassius, at the door, who does desire to see you."

"Is he alone?"

"No, sir, there are more with him."

Brutus' brow raised in only mild surprise. "Do you know them?"

Lucius shook his head. "No, sir; their hats are plucked about their ears, and half their faces buried in their cloaks, that by no means I may recognize them by any familiar feature."

Brutus nodded his understanding and said, "Let them enter."

2

Multiple sources have Lucius reporting that fifteen *days of March have passed ("Sir, March is wasted fifteen days."). However, The Yale Shakespeare has it as* fourteen *days, and their Notes argue that, if fifteen days have gone by, then this would now be the* Sixteenth *of March, the day* after *the ides of March – thus nullifying the soothsayer's prophecy. As I agree with The Yale Shakespeare's position on this matter, I chose to follow their version of the exchange.*

Once more, Lucius bowed and rushed from the orchard.

They are the conspirator faction, Brutus knew. *Oh, conspiracy, are you ashamed to show your dangerous brow by night, when evils are most free? Oh, then, by day where will you find a cavern dark enough to mask your monstrous face?*

Seek none, conspiracy. Hide it in smiles and affability; for if you proceed with your natural semblance shown, not even the gloomy path into Hades itself would be dim enough to hide you from prevention.

Brutus again heard footfalls, many this time. A group of men strode into the orchard – a half-dozen men, but only their leader, Cassius, was quick to approach Brutus.

"I think we are too bold upon your rest," Cassius greeted him. "Good morrow, Brutus; do we trouble you?"

Brutus shook his head. "I have been up this hour, awake all night." He looked around at the men who crowded about behind Cassius. "Do I know these men that come along with you?"

"Yes, every man of them;" Cassius assured him, "and there is no man here who does not honor you, and every one does wish you had that opinion of yourself which every noble Roman bears of you." He turned and gestured toward the man nearest him. "This is Trebonius."

Brutus nodded to Trebonius. "He is welcome here."

Cassius continued around the group. "This, Decius Brutus."

Brutus smiled at his distant cousin. "He is welcome, too."

"This, Casca; this, Cinna; and this, Metellus Cimber."

Brutus bowed all around. "They are all welcome." He passed his gaze upon each of them as he asked, "What wakeful cares do interpose themselves between your eyes and night?"

Cassius stepped closer to Brutus and lowered his voice. "Shall I entreat a word?"

Brutus nodded and allowed Cassius to lead him several strides away from the others, where the two men began a whispered conversation ...

Left to their own devices in Brutus' orchard, the other Romans shuffled a bit in awkward silence as they listened to the lingering wind and thunder, some of them watching the waning meteor shower. After a short time, Decius cleared his throat and inclined his head toward the horizon. "Here lies the east; does the day not break here?"

Casca responded to this with a simple, "No."

Cinna objected to Casca, "Oh, pardon, sir, it does; and yonder gray lines that interlace the clouds are messengers of day."

Casca seemed amused. "You shall confess that you are both deceived." Without warning, he drew his gladius from its sheath, startling the others into taking a collective step back. "Here, as I point my sword ..." He did so, indicating a different direction from the others. "... the sun arises, which is a great way encroaching on the south, considering the youthful season of the year." He lowered his sword, but did not resheath it. "Some two months hence, up higher toward the north, he first presents his fire, and the due east stands, as the Capitol, directly ..." The tip of his sword rose again. "... *here*." And that point marked, not only the east and the Capitol, but the returning Brutus, with Cassius a step behind him.

Brutus reached out toward them. "Give me your hands all over, one by one."

Cassius followed, "And let us swear our resolution."

"No, not an oath!" Brutus scolded, to the surprise of all – especially Cassius. As he shook each of their hands in turn, he continued, "If not the face of our fellow men, the suffering of our souls, the time's abuse – if these are weak motives, let us break off now, and every man return to his empty bed; so let haughty tyranny range on, till each man drops by his arbitrary whim." He let that soak in, then pressed on. "But if these things – as I am sure they do – bear enough fire to kindle cowards, and to steel with valor the melting spirits of women, *then*, countrymen, why should we need any spur but our own cause to propel us to redress? What other bond than resolute Romans that have spoke the word and *will not* mislead? And what other oath than honor to honor engaged, that this shall be ... or we will *fall* for it? 'Swearing' is for priests and cowards and deceitful men, old feeble wretches, and such long-suffering souls that welcome wrongs; to *bad* causes swear such creatures as men would doubt ... but do not stain the steadfast virtue of *our* enterprise, nor the irrepressible mettle of *our* spirits, to think that either our cause or our performance did need an oath – when every drop of blood that every Roman bears, and nobly bears, is guilty of an individual bastardy if he does break the smallest particle of any promise that has passed from him."

Many among them nodded their heartfelt agreement with this sentiment, but when Cassius next spoke, he segued, "But what of Cicero? Shall we sound him out? I think he will stand very strong with us."

Casca opined, "Let us not leave him out."

"No, by no means," Cinna agreed.

Metellus advocated further, and with zeal, "Oh, let us have him; for his silver hairs will purchase us a good opinion, and buy men's voices to commend our deeds. It shall be said *his* judgment ruled our hands – no speck of our youths and wildness shall appear, but all be buried in his gravity."

The group seemed in agreement, but after brief consideration, Brutus shook his head. "Oh, do not name him; let us not share our intentions with him, for he will never follow anything that other men begin."

Cassius shrugged. "Then leave him out."

Casca's assessment shifted as well. "Indeed, he is not fit."

Decius, however, raised a new concern: "Shall no other man be touched, but *only* Caesar?"

Cassius offered him a hard grin. "Decius, well urged." He then addressed them all, but favored Brutus. "I think it is not fitting that Mark Antony – so well beloved of Caesar – should outlive Caesar. We shall find in him a shrewd contriver; and, you know, his means, if he were to make the most of them, may well stretch so far as to injure us all; to prevent this, let Antony and Caesar fall together."

Before any of the others could voice their thoughts on the fate of Antony, Brutus again shook his head and offered the harsh proclamation, "Our course will seem too *bloody*, Caius Cassius, to cut the head off and then hack the limbs – like wrath in death, and then spite afterwards; for Antony is nothing but a limb of Caesar. Let us be sacrificers, but not butchers, Caius."

Brutus took a calming breath, then addressed the group.

"We all stand up against the spirit of Caesar, and in the spirit of men there is no blood. Oh, if only we could then come by Caesar's spirit and not dismember Caesar himself! But, alas, Caesar must bleed for it. And, gentle friends, let's kill him boldly, but *not* wrathfully. Let's carve him as a dish fit for the gods, *not* cut him as a carcass fit for hounds. And let our hearts, as subtle masters do, stir up their servants to an act of rage, and afterward seem to chide them. This shall make our purpose necessary, and *not* envious – when appearing so to the common eyes, we shall be called surgical purgers, *not* murderers."

While the others nodded along with his sage advice, Brutus once more directed his words to Cassius.

"And, for Mark Antony, do not think of him, for he can do no more than Caesar's arm when Caesar's head is off."

But Cassius objected, "And yet I fear him, for in the deep-rooted love he bears to Caesar—"

"Alas, good Cassius, *do not* think of him. If he loves Caesar, all that he can do affects himself – grow despondent and die for Caesar." Brutus then offered a knowing smile. "And that much is not likely, for he is given to sports, to wildness, and much company."

Trebonius agreed, "There is nothing to fear in him. Let him not die, for he will live and laugh at this afterward."

Before Cassius could offer any further rebuttals on the topic of Mark Antony, the clock struck.

"Quiet," Brutus said, "count the clock."

When the clock fell silent once more, Cassius commented, "The clock has struck three."

Trebonius grunted. "It is time to depart."

The others moved to do just that, until Cassius stopped and raised another concern. "But it is yet doubtful whether Caesar will come forth today or not; for he has grown superstitious of late, quite different from the strong opinion he once held of fantasy, of dreams, and fortune-telling ceremonies." He gestured toward the sky. "It may be these manifesting prodigies, the unaccustomed terror of this night, and the persuasion of his divining augurers may keep him from the Capitol today."

Decius stepped forward. "Never fear that. If he is so resolved, I can oversway him; for he loves to hear that unicorns may be trapped with trees, and bears with mirrors, elephants with pitfalls, lions with nets, and *men* with flatterers. But when I tell him he hates flatterers, he says he does, while *being* most flattered." When others chuckled at that, Decius continued, "Let me work him; for I can give his mood the true direction, and I will bring him to the Capitol."

"Nay," Cassius said in a low voice, "we will *all* of us be there to fetch him."

Brutus nodded. "By the eighth hour, is that the latest?"

"Let that be the latest," Cinna agreed, "and do not fail."

As they nodded all around on this and drifted to exit the orchard, Metellus observed, "Caius Ligarius does bear Caesar with difficulty, who berated him for speaking well of Pompey; I wonder that none of you have thought to include him."

Brutus acknowledged, "Now, good Metellus, go along by Ligarius' home. He loves me well, and I have given him reasons. Send him here, and I'll fashion him."

Cassius declared, "The morning comes upon us. We'll leave you, Brutus. And, friends, disperse yourselves; but all remember what you have said, and show yourselves true Romans."

Brutus escorted them out of his orchard. "Good gentlemen, look fresh and merrily; do not let our looks reveal our purposes, but bear it as our Roman actors do, with untired spirits and dignified demeanor. And so good morrow to you, every one."

The men all muttered their well wishes in return, and in short order, Brutus found himself once more alone in his orchard. Alone, indeed – it occurred to him that he had not seen Lucius in some time.

"Boy!" he called. "Lucius!"

The boy did not appear, nor respond.

"Fast asleep?" he murmured with envy. "It is no matter. Enjoy the honey-heavy dew of slumber. You have no imaginings nor no fantasies, which busy care draws in the brains of men. Therefore you sleep so sound ..."

But then Brutus heard movement from within the manor. Was Lucius awake after all?

Except it was not his servant who entered the orchard.

It was his beloved wife, Portia. "Brutus, my lord."

Brutus stood frozen, struggling to prevent his mouth from falling agape. When had Portia awoken? What had she heard? This was dark, bloody business, and he sought to neither upset nor endanger her.

Coming back to himself, he approached her. "Portia, what is the meaning of this? Why do you rise now? It is not good for your health in this manner, to commit your weak condition to the raw cold morning."

"Nor for yours, neither," Portia retorted, and Brutus knew that his wife would not be dismissed. "Brutus, you've discourteously stole from my bed; and yesternight at supper you suddenly arose and walked about, musing and sighing, with your arms crossed; and when I asked you what the matter was, you stared upon me with ungentle looks."

Brutus turned away, realizing too late how transparent his consternation had been. He drifted from his beloved wife, but determined, she trailed after him.

"I urged you further;" she continued, "then you scratched your head and, too impatiently, stamped with your foot. Yet I insisted; yet you did not answer, but with an angry wave of your hand gave sign for me to leave you. So I did, fearing to strengthen that impatience which seemed too much enkindled, nevertheless hoping it was but an effect of ill-humor – which sometimes has his hour with every man."

Portia reached out, taking Brutus by the arm and ending his passive retreat. Still he avoided meeting her gaze; and still she pressed him further.

"This 'ill-humor' will not let you eat nor talk nor sleep, and if it could work so much upon your body as it has much prevailed on your state of mind ... I would not *know* you, Brutus." Portia reached up and took his face in her hands, forcing Brutus to look at her. "My dear lord, make me acquainted with your cause of grief."

Brutus took her hands under his own and – with care and love – pulled them away from his cheeks. "I am not well in health," he lied, "and that is all." He tried to smile, but could feel its partial success.

Portia was not fooled for an instant. "Brutus is wise," she stated, "and were he not in health, he would embrace the means to come by it."

"Why, so I do," he said with more weight that intended. Still holding her hands, he kissed her fingers. "Good Portia, go to bed." He released her and stepped away again to sit upon a bench, taking care to keep his posture at ease.

Still Portia persisted. "*Is* Brutus sick? And is it healthful to walk uncovered and suck up the dampness of the dank morning? What, *is* Brutus sick, and will he steal out of his wholesome bed to dare the vile contagion of the night, and tempt the chilled air – still unpurified by the morning sun – to add to his sickness?" She shook her head with vehemence. "No, my Brutus, you have some 'sick' trouble within your *mind*, which – by the right and virtue of my place – I ought to know of."

Moving to the bench herself, Portia knelt before him, placing her hands upon his thighs.

"And upon my knees I entreat you, by my once commended beauty, by all your vows of love, and that great vow which did incorporate and make us *one*, that you make known to me – your self, your other half – why you are heavy-hearted, and what men tonight have had resort to you; for here have been some six or seven who did hide their faces even from darkness."

Brutus resisted scowling at what she had witnessed, which was far too much. He again tried smiling, and again fell short, as he took her by the arms and, rising himself, drew her to her feet. "Do not kneel, gentle Portia."

"I should not need to," she returned, "if you were gentle Brutus. Within the bond of marriage, tell me, Brutus ..." And this time it was she who retreated from him. "Is it excepted I should know no secrets that pertain to you? Am I your 'self' but, as it were, only with limitations? To keep with you at meals, comfort your bed, and talk to you sometimes? Do I dwell only in the periphery of your good pleasure?" She turned back, and her voice took on a harsher tone as she declared: "If it is nothing more, then Portia is Brutus' *harlot*, not his *wife*."

At these words, Brutus could no longer hold his distance; he hurried forward to take her into his arms, stroking her long hair beneath a loving hand. "You are my true and honorable wife," he assured her, "as dear to me as are the red drops that visit my sad heart."

"If this were true," she stated, remaining stiff within his embrace, "then I should know this secret. I grant I am a woman, but nevertheless a woman that Lord Brutus took to wife. I grant I am a woman, but nevertheless a woman well reputed, daughter of Cato of Utica – known for his high principles and integrity of conduct." At last, she relaxed into her husband's arms, encompassing him with her own. "Do you think I am no stronger than my sex, being so fathered and so husbanded? Tell me your secrets, I will not disclose them."

When Brutus hesitated still, Portia lowered an arm so that she could place her hand upon her leg.

"I have made strong proof of my reliability," she reminded him, "giving myself a voluntary wound here, in the thigh."

Brutus resisted the urge to flinch. He required no remembrance of the time Portia had slashed her thigh with a razor, then suffered a terrible fever from the infection. He knew she cited this scar to him, now, as proof positive of how well she – as a proud Roman matron – could endure pain, and that even torture would fail to wring his confidences from her.

"Can I bear *that* with patience," she demanded, echoing his thoughts, "and *not* my husband's secrets?"

Brutus looked upon her, into her eyes, shining so bright in the torchlight. *Oh, you gods,* he thought, *render me worthy of this noble wife!*

He should tell her; her counsel was strong and wise, as he so well knew. He had been a fool to think of leaving her out of this, danger or no. He told the others that they would proceed with this abscission, but if Portia drew a different conclusion ...

Brutus opened his mouth to speak, to share all with her—

A knock sounded from without, shattering the moment.

After an awkward pause, Brutus said, "Hark, hark! One knocks."

She held her ground still, imploring him with her eyes.

"Portia, go in awhile, and soon your bosom shall partake the secrets of my heart. All my commitments I will explain to you, all the writings upon my sad brows." He kissed her, then requested, "Leave me with haste."

At first, Portia looked as though she might argue further, might insist upon remaining by his side in greeting this latest visitation ... but then she lowered her eyes, nodded, and left him alone in the orchard.

Brutus felt torn by this success, and called with some force, "Lucius, who is it that knocks?"

Lucius had indeed awakened once more and appeared in short order with a hooded man in tow, the latter of whom also wore a kerchief wrapped around his face.

"Here is a sick man," the sleepy boy announced, referring to the cloth that shielded others from the guest's ailment, "that would speak with you."

The "sick" man reached up, threw back his hood, and pulled down the front of the kerchief, exposing his face for Brutus to see.

Brutus recognized him in an instant. *Caius Ligarius, that Metellus spoke of.*

Approaching them, Brutus nodded his head toward Lucius' quarters and told him, "Boy, stand aside."

Lucius bowed with gratitude and slipped out of the orchard.

"Caius Ligarius," Brutus greeted, "how are you?"

Ligarius smiled as he lifted the cloth back over his nose and mouth. "Please receive 'good morrow' from a feeble tongue."

Brutus nodded his acceptance. "Oh, what a time you have chosen, brave Caius, to wear a kerchief!" He gestured for the man to sit upon the nearby bench. "I wish you were not sick!"

"I am not sick," Ligarius protested, even as he eased himself with shaky legs onto the bench, "if Brutus has in hand any exploit worthy of the name of 'honor'."

"Such an exploit I have in hand, Ligarius," Brutus assured him, "if you had a healthful ear to hear of it."

Ligarius rallied back to his feet at once. "By all the gods that Romans bow before, I hereby discard my sickness." With as much flourish as he could muster, he removed the kerchief from his face. Smiling upon Brutus, he declared, "Soul of Rome! Brave son derived from honorable loins! You, like an exorcist, have conjured up my deadened spirit. Now bid me run, and I will strive with things impossible – yea, get the better of them. What am I to do?"

Brutus placed his hand upon the man's shoulder. "A piece of work that will make sick men whole."

Ligarius offered a knowing smile. "But are not some 'whole' that we must make sick?"

Brutus nodded. "That must we also. What it is, my Caius, I shall unfold to you, as we are going, to whom it must be done."

"Set on your foot, and with a heart new-fired I follow you, to do I do not know what; but it suffices that *Brutus* leads me on."

In the distance, thunder rolled yet again. Brutus pondered this timing, and also the fact that he had been so close to sharing this business with Portia – indeed, had promised to do so. Yet, here before him awaited the next step in this monumental task. Should he send Ligarius away for the time being and return to his wife, to seek her counsel ...?

Expectant, Ligarius stared at him, waiting for him to lead.

The thunder's final echoes faded away.

At last, Brutus said to Ligarius, "Follow me then." And he led the man to his study.

PART TWO

CHAPTER TWO

The night's terrors, though decreasing by degrees, were not altogether departed. Their weighty portents lingered over all of Rome.

Including the great house of Julius Caesar.

In their chambers, his wife Calphurnia continued to moan, to thrash, to exclaim in her sleep. Caesar, clasping his nightgown close about his chest, looked on from the doorway. He watched his disturbed wife, and brooded.

Nor heaven nor Earth have been at peace tonight, he fretted. *Calphurnia has cried out three times in her sleep, "Help ho, they murder Caesar!"*

As if sensing his thoughts, Calphurnia issued another ragged outburst, but these words were too garbled for Caesar to interpret them.

Interpret ...

Turning, Caesar fled from their—

(No. Not "fled." Caesar never "fled"!)

Caesar *strode* from their chambers into the common room, calling out, "Who's within?"

In an instant, a servant appeared. "My lord?"

Ensuring that his voice remained steadfast, Caesar ordered, "Go bid the priests do an immediate sacrifice, and bring me their opinions of the outcome."

The servant bowed, turning to obey even as he said, "I will, my lord." In seconds, the man was gone from sight.

Caesar stood rock-still a moment, his head high and proud. By the gods, he was Caesar! He should not allow himself—

In spite of everything, movement from behind startled him. He whirled to find, much to his surprise, his wife – her eyes bloodshot, her cheeks ashen – standing in the doorway to their chambers, one hand clutching it to steady herself.

"What do you intend, Caesar?" Calphurnia gasped. "Do you think to walk forth?" She lowered her bracing hand, shook her head as though to clear away the fog, and sharpened her posture to match his. In a much firmer tone, she stated, "You shall not stir out of your house today."

Pride recapturing the reins of his temperament, Caesar held his head higher still. "Caesar *shall* go forth. The things that threatened me never looked but on my back; when they shall see the *face* of Caesar, they are vanished."

Realizing her error, that imperiousness was not the means by which to win this battle, Calphurnia eased her demeanor and her words as she approached him. "Caesar, I never heeded omens, yet now they frighten me. Besides the things that we have heard and seen, there is one within," she gestured toward the servants' quarters, "who recounts most horrid sights seen by the watchmen: A lioness has birthed a whelp in the streets, and graves have yawned and yielded up their dead; fierce fiery warriors fought upon the clouds in ranks and squadrons and regular formations of war, which drizzled blood upon the Capitol. The noise of battle clashed in the air, horses did neigh, and dying men did groan, and ghosts did shriek and squeal about the streets."

When Caesar made no reply to any of this, Calphurnia approached and placed her pleading hands upon his arms.

"Oh, Caesar, these things are beyond all experience, and I do *fear* them."

Caesar looked down upon her and spoke, his tone softer but his words firm, "What can be avoided whose end is purposed by the mighty gods?" He offered a smile, but it served her no comfort as he continued, "Yet Caesar shall go forth, for these predictions are as applicable to the world in general as to Caesar."

She retorted, "When beggars die there are no comets seen; the heavens themselves blaze forth the death of *princes*."

Caesar's chin lifted once more. "Cowards die many times before their deaths; the *valiant* never taste of death but once." Then he willed himself to calm and returned to his gentle tone. "Of all the wonders that I have yet heard," he told her, "it seems to me most strange that men should fear death – seeing that death, a necessary end, will come when it will come."

Before Calphurnia, tears of frustration in her reddened eyes, could respond, the servant returned and bowed. He appeared quite agitated, and in spite of the early morning chill, sweat stood out upon his forehead.

Caesar looked to him and demanded, "What do the divining augurers say?"

The servant repeated his bow as he reported in a trembling voice, "They would not have you stir forth today." He looked up to his master and, swallowing hard, continued, "Plucking forth the entrails of an offering ... they could not find a heart within the beast."

Calphurnia gasped, her hands tightening on Caesar's arms. Even Caesar's pulse quickened upon hearing these words, though he would never have admitted it. In irritation, he waved the servant away.

As much to himself as to his wife, Caesar proclaimed, "The gods do this in shame of cowardice. Caesar should be a beast without a heart if he should stay at home today for fear." His own words satisfied him. "No, Caesar shall not. Danger knows full well that Caesar is more dangerous than he. We are two lions littered in one day, and *I* the elder and more terrible." He nodded, a determined gesture. "And Caesar *shall* go forth."

Caesar made to pull away from Calphurnia, but she would not release him. "Alas, my lord, your wisdom is consumed in overconfidence. Do not go forth today!" When she observed that he was still adamant, she suggested, "Call it *my* fear that keeps you in the house, and not your own." Then another idea occurred to her. "We'll send Mark Antony to the Senate-House, and he shall say you are not well today." She released him at last, but only so that she could kneel before him and beg, "Let me, upon my knee, prevail in this."

Gazing down at her, Caesar released a long sigh, then reached down to take her pleading hands. "Mark Antony shall say I am not well; and, for your whim, I will stay at home."

Calphurnia panted as though from holding a long breath, and smiled in relief as Caesar drew her back to her feet and into his arms.

And there she would have been content to remain, save for the interruption of her husband's next words.

"Here's Decius Brutus," Caesar said, "*he* shall tell them so."

Calphurnia looked around to see their servant leaving as, indeed, the cousin of Marcus Brutus entered their common room.

"Caesar, all hail!" the man called with a smile as he approached. "Good morrow, worthy Caesar. I come to fetch you to the Senate-House."

Caesar released his wife, but remained by her side. "And you have come in very opportune time to bear my greeting to the Senators, and tell them that I will not come today." As Decius halted in surprise, Caesar stressed, " 'Cannot' is false; and that I 'dare' not, falser. I *will not* come today. Tell them so, Decius."

Decius wore a strange expression upon his face, so Calphurnia tried to help by suggesting, "Say he is sick."

In spite of his prior agreement, her husband's back stiffened. "Shall Caesar send a *lie*?" he snapped. "Have I, in conquest, stretched my arm so far, only to be afraid to tell graybeards the truth?" He turned back to their guest. "Decius, go tell them Caesar *will not* come."

Decius smiled, and it bore a quality which Calphurnia did not care for, yet could not label. "Most mighty Caesar," he said, "let me know some cause, otherwise I would be laughed at when I tell them so."

Caesar moved toward him, leaving his wife and raising his voice. "The cause is in my *will*: I - will - not - come. *That* is enough to satisfy the Senate." But once he stood before his guest, Caesar said in a friendlier manner, "But for your private satisfaction, because I love you, I will let you know: Calphurnia here, my wife, keeps me at home. She dreamt last night that she saw my statue, which – like a fountain with a hundred spouts – did run pure blood; and many lusty Romans came smiling and did bathe their hands in it." He glanced back at Calphurnia and smirked. "And for these she does apply warnings and portents and imminent evils, and on her knee has begged that I will stay at home today."

Decius considered this; he rubbed his chin in thought as he approached Calphurnia, then he began a slow nod, which gained speed as he spoke to her, "This dream is all misinterpreted. It was a fair and *fortunate* vision." He turned back to Caesar. "Your statue spouting blood in many pipes, in which so many smiling Romans bathed, signifies that – from *you* – great Rome shall suck reviving blood, and that great men shall crowd for healing tinctures, assimilating stains, religious relics, and heraldic emblems of Caesar." He spread his arms wide in grandiosity. "*This*, by Calphurnia's dream, is signified."

To Calphurnia's dismay, Caesar appeared quite pleased by this. He declared to Decius, "And this way you have well expounded it."

Calphurnia parted her lips to speak, but Decius cut her off. "I have, when you have heard what I can say; and know it now: The Senate have concluded to give, this day, a crown to mighty Caesar!"

Caesar lit up like the morning sun, approaching his wife with a pleased glint in his eyes, even as Calphurnia felt a chill run down her spine.

But Decius was not yet finished. "If you shall send them word you will not come, their minds may change. Besides, it would be a gibe likely to be rendered, for someone to say 'Break up the Senate till another time, when Caesar's *wife* shall meet with better dreams.' If Caesar hides himself, shall they not whisper, 'Look, Caesar is *afraid*'?"

That did not sit well with Caesar, not at all. He rounded upon Decius, the pleased glint replaced by sharp ire.

Decius was swift to raise a placating hand and bow. "Pardon me, Caesar," he offered in submission, "for my dear, dear love to your advancement bids me tell you this, and reason is subservient to my love."

Caesar's mood teetered for a moment, but then he revealed himself to have been satisfied when he turned to his wife and proclaimed, "How foolish do your fears seem now, Calphurnia! I am ashamed I did yield to them. Give me my robe, for I will go."

Calphurnia wanted to argue with Caesar – no, she wanted to beg, to scream at him in fear and desperation beyond words! But a gentle commotion drew her attention past her husband, and she saw more than a half-dozen men entering their common room.

Caesar followed her gaze. "And look, here is Publius, come to fetch me."

Indeed, Publius stood at the front of the group, which included Marcus Brutus, Ligarius, Metellus, Casca, Trebonius, and Cinna. Being first so addressed, Publius called, "Good morning, Caesar."

Defeated, Calphurnia's shoulders drooped, along with her heart, as she fetched her husband's robe as requested.

Meanwhile, Caesar strode toward the group in magnanimous fashion. "Welcome, Publius. What, Brutus, are you stirred so early, too?" Brutus inclined his head. "Good morning, Casca. Caius Ligarius, Caesar was never so much your enemy as that same fever which has made you lean." Caesar then looked over the group. "What is it o'clock?"

Brutus answered, "Caesar, it has struck eight."

Caesar smiled and addressed them all, "I thank you for your pains and courtesy." Then, like Calphurnia before him, Caesar looked past the assemblage toward the entrance, and they all turned to the newcomer ... and more than one of them stiffened at the revelation.

"See," Caesar called as his servant led in Mark Antony, "Antony, that revels all night long, is notwithstanding *up*." He raised his hand to his friend. "Good morning, Antony."

Antony bowed his head. "So to most noble Caesar."

To his servant, Caesar gestured toward the atrium and ordered, "Bid them prepare within."

The servant bowed and rushed off to make it so.

Calphurnia then returned with Caesar's robe. He moved to her, and as she helped him dress, he commented, "I am to blame to be so waited for."

Calphurnia said nothing to that, merely continued helping her husband prepare for his day.

"Now, Cinna;" Caesar spoke louder, "now, Metellus; what, Trebonius: I have an hour's talk in store for you. Remember that you call on me today; be near me that I may remember you."

Aloud, Trebonius answered, "Caesar, I will." But within, he thought, *And so near will I be that your best friends shall wish I had been further.*

"Good friends," Caesar gestured toward the atrium, "go in, and taste some wine with me, and we – like friends! – will straightway go together."

Upon this invitation, all of them moved toward the atrium – even Calphurnia, though she did so with a heavy heart and qualms within her belly.

Brutus brought up the rear, masking the frown which sought to spread across his face as he pondered Caesar's phrase, "like friends."

That every 'like' is not the same, oh, Caesar, he thought, *the heart of Brutus grieves to think upon.*

PART TWO

CHAPTER THREE

In these glorious days of Rome, many citizens ambled near the Capitol when rumor held that the great Julius Caesar might attend the Senate-House; the streets sprung to life at the earliest signs of dawn, and the hopeful audience would wait all the morning long. And so it was this day, too, as word had spread that Caesar would indeed be in attendance, and not even the terrible night's ghastly wonders could stem the tide.

But Caesar's attendance was not the only word to spread in recent hours. Some had been privy to darker tidings.

Approaching the steps leading to the Capitol, Artemidorus of Cnidos – that most notable teacher of rhetoric, who had schooled many members of the Senate in the skills of oration – drew forth from his robes a small scroll. Glancing around with as much forced ease as he could bring himself to portray, he unrolled the parchment and studied his own words, which he had written less than an hour ago:

Caesar, beware of Brutus; take heed of Cassius; come not near Casca; have an eye to Cinna; trust not Trebonius; mark well Metellus Cimber; Decius Brutus loves you not; you have wronged Caius Ligarius. There is but one mind in all these men, and it is bent against Caesar. If you are not immortal, look about you. Overconfidence gives way to conspiracy. The mighty gods defend you!

> *Your friend,*
> *Artemidorus*

Nodding to himself, satisfied that this was the most concise way to communicate the danger he had overheard – from some of his own brash, former students, no less! – and wished to share with noble Caesar.

But how best to deliver the message to Caesar, without rousing suspicions from those who already planned appalling violence?

After several long seconds of consideration, Artemidorus chose to mount the Capitol steps, but halted his climb roughly halfway to the top.

Here I will stand till Caesar passes along, and – as a petitioner – I will give him this. My heart laments that virtue cannot live free from the bite of jealous rivalry!

If you read this, oh, Caesar, you may yet live.

If not ... the Fates do conspire with traitors.

And so Artemidorus stood his ground ... and waited.

PART TWO

CHAPTER FOUR

Portia was beside herself.

Brutus had continued his counsel with his visitors into the morning hours, so that Portia, in spite of her best efforts, had fallen back asleep. And when she had awakened once more, she was alone, her husband never having returned to their bed.

She had no facts, nothing grounded upon which to base her anxiety, but she had overheard enough snippets of her husband's conversations to speculate on the severity of this day. A myriad of possibly innocent – perhaps even virtuous! – explanations for Brutus' behavior and his cavalcade of visitors last night were considered and dismissed almost before they could form in her mind.

Without conscious thought, Portia found herself standing on the street before the home she shared with Brutus, and as she wrung her hands, she called for Lucius.

Once Lucius arrived and bowed before her, she ordered, "I ask you, boy, run to the Senate-House. Do not stay to answer me, but get you gone." When the boy hesitated, she demanded, "Why do you stay?"

Lucius was at a loss. "To know my errand, madam."

Portia shook her head and waved her hands in angst. "I would have had you there, and here again, before I can tell you what you shall do there."

Oh, faithfulness, she thought, *be strong upon my side; set a huge mountain between my heart and tongue! I have a man's mind, but a woman's might. How hard it is for women to keep a secret!*

When she realized that the idiot boy stood before her, waiting, she snapped, "Are you still here?"

Lucius' cheeks flushed, and his eyes hinted at tears of angst. "Madam, what shall I *do*? Run to the Capitol, and nothing else? And so return to you, and nothing else?"

Portia knew that she was treating the boy in unfair fashion, and forced herself to soften her words as best she could. "Yes, bring me word, boy, if your lord looks well, for he went sickly forth." Then she added, "And take good note what *Caesar* does, what suitors approach him."

Then Portia jolted with such intensity that Lucius retreated a step.

"Hark, boy," she gasped, "what noise is that?"

Lucius looked about himself. "I hear none, madam."

But Portia, her eyes wide, persisted, "Please, listen well. I heard a tumultuous noise like a fray, and the wind brings it from the Capitol."

Lucius held his breath for several seconds, doing his best to perform as asked. But still he reported, "Truly, madam, I hear nothing."

Portia rounded on the boy, her face contorted in misplaced anger, but then something beyond him ensnared her attention.

A ramshackle derelict was shuffling by, dragging one leg but moving with a determined gait nonetheless. The sorry fellow looked familiar to Portia, someone she had seen not so long ago ...

Yes! She *had* seen him – last month, during the Feast of Lupercal! He had been the soothsayer who warned Caesar to ...

To beware the ides of March.

Portia's heart raced ever faster as she called out, "Come here, fellow."

The soothsayer fixed his one good eye upon her, hesitated, then drew nearer. Normally, Portia might have balked at the approach of such a decrepit man, but not this day.

She asked him, "Which way have you been?"

The soothsayer shrugged, and with a polite smile answered, "At mine own house, good lady."

Portia wondered what "house" this poor fellow might possess, but let that be. "What is it o'clock?"

"About the ninth hour, lady."

"Has Caesar yet gone to the Capitol?"

The soothsayer shook his dirty head. "Madam, not yet; I go to take my stand, to see him pass on to the Capitol."

"You have some petition to Caesar, have you not?"

The soothsayer hesitated again, then nodded. "That I have, lady: If it will please Caesar to be so good *to* Caesar as to hear me, I shall implore him to befriend himself."

Portia swallowed against her gorge rising in her throat. "Why, do you know any harm is intended towards him?"

"None that I know will be, much that I fear may chance." He glanced around, then bowed to her. "Good morning to you. Here the street is narrow; the throng that follows Caesar at his heels, of Senators, of Praetors, common petitioners, will crowd a feeble man almost to death. I'll get me to a place more open, and there speak to great Caesar as he comes along."

Portia opened her mouth to say more, but the soothsayer shuffled along his way without a backward glance.

Releasing her drawn breath as a sigh, she said in defeat, "I must go in." Then, her head aching, her eyes burning, she whispered, "Woe to me! How weak a thing the heart of woman is! Oh, Brutus, may the heavens speed you in your enterprise!"

She barely withheld a gasp as she turned and saw Lucius watching her, his eyes wide in alarm.

Surely, the boy heard me! She had not intended to speak aloud of this, but in truth, she had forgotten that he was there.

To Lucius, she explained, "Brutus has a petition that Caesar will not grant."

Lucius offered a slight nod in reply, but his countenance remained confused and anxious.

Oh, I grow faint. "Run, Lucius, and praise me to my lord. Say ... I am merry. Then come to me again, and bring me word of what he does say to you."

Finally given a solid command he could grasp, Lucius bowed and, with clear relief, hurried down the street toward the Senate-House.

Portia closed her eyes a moment ... then, holding herself erect with perhaps too much rigor, she returned to her house.

PART THREE

CHAPTER ONE

Julius Caesar's passage to the Capitol had been intended, more or less, as an informal affair. And yet, as he and his entourage approached the Senate-House, the trumpeters had nonetheless scrambled into position along the sides of the front steps, and a flourish sounded through the morning air as Caesar led them to their final destination.

Final, that is, save one last development: Caesar spotted a familiar figure standing near the bottom of the stairs, and recalled the "warning" the sad fellow had offered him during the Feast of Lupercal. A smile crossed Caesar's lips as he deviated his course and approached the soothsayer who had borne such ill tidings, and his escorts followed.

With defiant pride, Caesar said to the haggard fellow, "The ides of March are come."

The soothsayer's good eye met his gaze. "Aye, Caesar, but *not gone*."

Caesar could not have stated exactly what response he had desired or expected, but this was not it. He was tempted to exchange chilled glances with one of the others – perhaps dear Antony or Brutus – but stubborn determination against sharing any apprehension drew a blank veil across his features. The soothsayer looked as though he wished to speak further, but Caesar turned from him as though no words at all had passed between them, and mounted the stairs to the Senate-House.

Halfway through his ascent, a voice called, "Hail, Caesar!"

Caesar had heard many "Hail, Caesars" that morning, of course, but this particular voice stood out in its familiarity. He glanced over and recognized Artemidorus at once.

With some urgency, the renowned teacher of rhetoric offered a scroll to him. "Read this document."

Curious, Caesar reached out to accept the scroll—

In the blink of an eye, Decius Brutus stood between them. He drew his own scroll from within his robes and spoke as though he had just recalled a task. "Trebonius does desire you to read over this humble petition, at your best leisure."

But Artemidorus raised his voice in sudden desperation. "Oh, Caesar, read mine *first*; for mine's a petition that touches Caesar nearer." His hand shook as he proffered the scroll once again, almost waving it in Caesar's face. "*Read it*, great Caesar."

The man's presumption irritated Caesar. "What touches me, myself, shall be *last* attended."

"Do not delay, Caesar," Artemidorus begged, "read it *instantly*."

Quite put off by this public display from Artemidorus, Caesar made a show of looking around at his retinue. "What," Caesar scoffed, "is the fellow mad?"

"Sirrah," Publius scorned as he stepped forward to brush Artemidorus aside and away from Caesar, "make way."

Artemidorus appeared near tears as Caesar marched past him without accepting the warning he had written.

Cassius halted to address the man. "What, you urge your petitions in the street? Come to the Capitol."

Artemidorus considered it ... then his shoulders sagged in defeat, and he descended the steps, away from the Senate-House.

As Cassius stared after him, another Senator – Popilius Lena – paused next to Cassius and said, "I wish your enterprise today may thrive."

Cassius blinked in surprise. "What 'enterprise,' Popilius?"

But Popilius merely replied, "Fare you well." He then hurried up the steps after Caesar.

Brutus appeared at Cassius' side. "What did Popilius Lena say?"

Cassius replied in a low voice, "He wished today our 'enterprise' might thrive. I fear our purpose is discovered."

Brutus inclined his head toward the landing at the top of the steps. "Look how he makes his way to Caesar. Mark him."

Cassius looked up and saw that Popilius was indeed approaching and calling to Caesar; the latter turned back and waited to hear what the Senator had to say.

Sweat forming upon his brow, Cassius turned and waved Casca forward. When their confederate approached, Cassius gestured to Popilius and urged, "Casca, be swift, for we fear prevention."

Casca understood the situation in a glance and mounted the steps toward Popilius with determination.

"Brutus," Cassius said with a shaky voice, "what shall be done? If this is known, Cassius *or* Caesar shall never turn back from here, for I will slay *myself*." He reached within his robes as though he intended to draw his hidden short-sword and commit suicide, here and now.

But Brutus grasped his forearm with a firm hand. "Cassius, be unmoved. Popilius Lena does not speak of our purposes, for look – he smiles, and Caesar does not change."

A long, tense breath escaped Cassius when he saw that Brutus was correct: Caesar even laughed as he and Popilius entered the Senate-House together.

Swallowing hard, Cassius nodded to Brutus, and was then pleased to share additional good tidings. "Trebonius knows his time, for look, Brutus." He pointed. "He draws Mark Antony out of the way."

They watched as Trebonius draped a friendly arm around Antony's shoulders, guiding the younger man from the Senate-House entrance and speaking to him with great enthusiasm on whatever topic he was sharing, their heads close as though it were an important subject indeed. Antony was nodding, and when he made as if to pause, Trebonius persisted. They continued their casual stroll ...

Taking Mark Antony away from Julius Caesar.

With a knowing look, Brutus and Cassius ascended the remaining steps and entered the Senate-House.

The pair had scarcely set foot inside before Decius approached them, his face no longer quite able to hide his tension. "Where is Metellus Cimber?" he whispered. "Let him go and presently offer his petition to Caesar."

"He is ready," Brutus assured him. "Press near and second him."

The other conspirators emboldened themselves, and one another, as they moved toward the midpoint of the chamber, closer to Caesar. Cinna drew near to Casca and murmured, "Casca, you are the first that rears your hand."

Casca licked his lips, his mouth too dry to speak, but he nodded his acknowledgment.

Taking his place among the center of them all, Caesar raised his voice and called, "Are we all ready? What is now amiss that Caesar and his Senate must redress?"

The other Senators, those not involved with their plot, settled back to watch proceedings unfold. But Brutus and Cassius exchanged another heavy look – Caesar's usage of "*his* Senate" provided final, damning validation of their collective concerns.

Metellus Cimber approached Caesar and knelt before him. "Most high, most mighty, and most powerful Caesar, Metellus Cimber throws before your seat a humble heart."

Caesar appeared surprised, but gratified, by Cimber's words and actions. Yet he proclaimed, "I must prevent you, Cimber. These prostrations and these low-bowing courtesies might fire the blood of ordinary men, and turn settled decisions into the arbitrary law of children's games."

He looked around at all the Senators. "Do not be so foolish as to think that *Caesar* bears such rebellious blood that will be thawed from true stability by that which melts other fools – I mean sweet words, low-bending courtesies, and base servile fawning."

With that, Caesar returned his attention to Cimber, and spoke with condescension. "Your brother, by decree, is banished. If you do bend and pray and fawn for him, I spurn you – like a cur – out of my way."

And he again addressed his general audience, "Know, Caesar does not wrong ... nor, without *cause*, will he be satisfied."

Still on his knees, Metellus made a great show of his dismay, spreading his arms to the assemblage and calling out, "Is there no voice more worthy than my own, to sound more sweetly in great Caesar's ear for the recalling of my banished brother?"

A low hubbub rolled through the Senators who stood confused by this extravagant behavior, but before it could gain momentum, it was silenced with a collective exclamation when Marcus Brutus himself knelt alongside Metellus.

To the further amazement of all, Brutus took Caesar's hand and kissed it. "I kiss your hand," he declared, "but not in 'flattery,' Caesar; desiring of you that Publius Cimber may have an immediate free recall."

Of everyone present, Caesar stood the most astonished among them. "What," he gasped in disbelief, "*Brutus*?"

And then it was Cassius who fell to his knees before the great *Dictator Perpetuo*. "Pardon, Caesar!" he pleaded. "Caesar, *pardon*! As low as to your foot does Cassius fall, to beg enfranchisement for Publius Cimber."

Caesar looked across the faces of the three men, as unsettled as he ever allowed himself to display. Then he rallied and stepped back, away from them.

"I could be well moved," he said, "if I were as *you*; if I could pray to move superiors, as you do, prayers would move me." He held his head high, looking down his nose at the three. "But *I* am constant as the Northern Star, of whose true-fixed and stable quality there is no equal in the heavens. The skies are painted with unnumbered sparks; they are all fire, and every one does shine ... but there is only *one* in all that does hold his place. So it is in the world; it is furnished well with men, and men are flesh and blood, and intelligent. Yet in all that number, I do know of only *one* that maintains his position, unshaked of motion ... and to demonstrate that *I* am he, let me show it a little, even in this:" Caesar held his head higher still. "That I was firm Cimber should be banished, and firm do I remain to keep him so."

Caesar's bearing and smug smile made it clear to all that he considered the matter closed. And so the pompous would-be-king was further astounded when Cinna joined the others on his knees ...

... and therefore gave little attention to Casca as he moved around to stand at Caesar's back.

Cinna was crying, "Oh, Caesar—!"

"Go hence!" Caesar barked, his cheeks reddening. "Will you lift up Mount Olympus?"

Then Decius joined the kneeling men, now forming a semicircle around Caesar. "Great Caesar—!"

Flabbergasted, Caesar gestured toward Brutus. "Does not even *Brutus* kneel in vain?"

Then the arc of men around Caesar fell quiet, even as the other Senators cried out. Caesar lifted his gaze, curious as to what prompted—

"Hands," Casca's bellow echoed throughout as he raged, "speak for me!"

The blade bit low into Julius Caesar's neck. Caesar whirled, groaning as the dagger ripped out of his flesh. Enraged even through his pain, he lunged for Casca's throat—

But then Cassius produced his sword, and its blade, too, found Caesar. As did Cinna's. And Decius'. And more still—

Mayhem erupted. Many of the Senators and their servants who stood apart from the conspirators panicked and fled, their screams of terror abounding.

The soothsayer's warnings echoing through his mind, his wife's pleas sounding through his heart, Caesar yearned to escape, but every direction he turned welcomed another dagger into his body. Blood, *his* blood, fell like rain to the Senate-House floor ...

When at last there came a pause to the deadly onslaught, Caesar found himself facing his friend, Marcus Brutus. He saw that Brutus, too, held a ready blade in his hand ... yet, unlike the hatred which overwhelmed the countenances of all his other attackers, Brutus offered an expression of pity, and regret.

Shuffling forward, Caesar reached out with trembling, bloody hands, grasping onto Brutus' robe for support.

Where Caesar had perceived clemency, he found none.

Sorrow still heavy in his eyes, his beloved friend met Caesar with a truly killing blow, the dagger driving up through his ribs and into his heart.

All physical pain fled Caesar, then; he perceived only a spreading chill. The sole remaining anguish stemmed from this final betrayal.

Caesar whispered, *"Et tu, Brutè?"*

Tears welled in Brutus' eyes, for he understood those Latin words: *And you, Brutus?*

Caesar wheezed out a concluding breath, commanding himself, "Then fall, Caesar!"

His hands slipped from Brutus, and he did fall to the Senate-House floor, onto the foot of the pedestal of Pompey's statue, dead.

"Liberty!" Cinna cried, his bloody dagger held aloft. "Freedom! Tyranny is dead!" He then called after the retreating Senators. "Run away, proclaim, cry it about the streets."

Cassius nodded, adding, "Some should go to the public pulpits and cry out, 'Liberty, freedom, and enfranchisement'!"

But to those others who remained within, Brutus raised his voice above their whimpers and moans. "People and Senators, do not be frightened; do not flee, stand still." He pointed his dagger to Caesar's body. "Ambition's debt is *paid*."

Before he could receive a response – indeed, if any were to be forthcoming – Casca stood sweating before him. "Go to the pulpit, Brutus."

"And Cassius, too," chimed Decius.

But Brutus remained otherwise focused. "Where's Publius?"

"Here," Cinna called, "quite confounded with this mutiny."

Brutus looked to find Cinna standing next to their fellow Senator; Publius, indeed, appeared frozen in shock.

Metellus brandished his dagger. "Stand fast together, in case some friend of Caesar's should chance—"

Brutus overrode him, "Do not talk of 'standing together.' " Keeping his own dagger pointed to the floor, he approached the stunned Senator. "Publius, be of good cheer. There is no harm intended to your person ..." and then he raised his voice further to add, "... nor to *no other Roman*. Tell them so, Publius."

Cassius joined him, keeping his own tone gentle. "And leave us, Publius, for fear that the people, rushing on *us*, should do your age some mischief."

Publius nodded in vague fashion, but his eyes had focused upon the blood – Caesar's blood – splashed on their robes.

Brutus spoke with care. "Do so ..." then he raised his voice yet again, "... and let no man pay the penalty for this deed but *we*, the doers."

Publius met Brutus' eyes, and this time the older man nodded with more confidence. He moved to exit the Senate-House, and all the remaining Senators and servants – save those who had conspired against Caesar – followed his example, leaving this terrible scene.

As the last of them departed, Trebonius pushed his way inside to join the others.

Cassius asked him, "Where is Antony?"

"Fled to his house, amazed." Trebonius shook his head. "Men, women, and children stare, cry out, and run as if it were doomsday."

Brutus sighed, finding himself staring upon Caesar. "Fates, we will soon know your pleasures." When the others looked to him, he continued, "That we shall die, we know; it is but the time, and drawing the remaining days out, that men worry upon."

Casca countered, "Why, he that cuts off twenty years of life cuts off that many years of fearing death." [3]

Brutus acquiesced, "Grant that, and then death is a benefit. So we are Caesar's friends, that have abridged his time of fearing death."

The others exchanged glances as Brutus approached Caesar's body. He stared down at it for a time, then knelt alongside it.

Looking up at the others, Brutus stated, "Stoop, Romans, stoop, and let us bathe our hands in Caesar's blood up to the elbows and smear our swords. Then we shall walk forth, even to the marketplace, and waving our red weapons over our heads, let's all cry 'Peace, freedom, and liberty'!"

The others hesitated at first, balking at the notion of actually "bathing" in Julius Caesar's blood. But then Cassius waved them forward as he moved to join Brutus. "Stoop then," he agreed, "and wash."

After a final wave of reluctance, the rest of the conspirators joined their leaders in this gruesome task.

As they soaked their hands and blades, Cassius encouraged them to higher spirits. "How many ages," he declared, "from this day forth, shall this – our lofty scene – be reenacted, in states yet-unborn and

---

3

Some versions of the play, as well as some film adaptations, attribute this line to Cassius, rather than Casca. In this instance, I followed the Riverside and Yale editions in assigning it to Casca.

accents yet-unknown!"

Brutus was unmoved by that sentiment. "How many times shall Caesar bleed in these reenactments, though he now lies outstretched on Pompey's pedestal, no worthier than the dust!"

When this gave the others further pause, Cassius countered, "So often as that shall be, so often shall the group of us be called 'the men that gave their country liberty.' "

In the end, the conspirators could settle upon no single emotion, so they bathed their hands and blades in silence ...

Finally, Decius asked, "What now, shall we go forth?"

"Aye," Cassius answered, "every man away from here. Brutus shall lead, and we will grace his heels with the most boldest and best hearts of Rome."

But Brutus was already standing, his hand gripping his dagger with renewed tension. "Quiet, who comes here?" The others turned, prepared to face treachery; even as they joined him on their feet, Brutus observed, "A friend of Antony's."

Indeed, a familiar servant had slipped into the Senate-House as they knelt around the spreading pool of Caesar's blood. The instant he realized the Senators had spotted him, he threw himself onto his knees, his head low, his hands trembling upon his thighs, and his voice no more steady for it.

"Like so, Brutus," the servant quavered, "my master did bid me kneel." He lowered his head further toward the floor. "Like so, Mark Antony did bid me fall down, and being prostrate, he bade me say this: 'Brutus is noble, wise, valiant, and honorable; Caesar was mighty, bold, royal, and loving.' Say, 'I love Brutus, and I honor him;' say, 'I feared Caesar, honored him, and loved him.' " The servant swallowed hard enough for all to hear, then raised his head, somewhat. "If Brutus will vouchsafe that Antony may *safely* come to him, and be convinced how Caesar has deserved to lie in death. Mark Antony shall not love Caesar dead so well as Brutus living, but will follow the fortunes and affairs of noble Brutus throughout the hazards of this precarious situation with all true faith. So says my master, Antony."

Holding his dagger low against his thigh, Brutus approached the servant and said, "Your master is a wise and valiant Roman; I never thought him worse. Tell him, if he is willing, come to this place, and he shall be convinced – and, by my honor, depart *untouched*."

The servant breathed a sigh of relief and rose to his feet, though his head remained low. "I'll fetch him at once." He then bowed from the waist and hurried from the Senate-House.

Satisfied by the exchange, Brutus' stance relaxed for the first time since their assault on Caesar. "I know that we shall have him as a good friend."

"I wish we may," Cassius retorted, his expression sharing his discontent as much as his tone. "But I still have a mind that fears him much, and my misgivings often prove only too well founded."

Brutus opened his mouth to offer his own rebuttal, but then the Senate-House door opened, not softly, but proudly, and as the newcomer stood with the morning shining in from behind him, all within recognized that silhouette.

Brutus drew a steadying breath. "But here comes Antony."

Mark Antony stepped inside, closing the large doors behind him. He strode forward toward the group, his face impassive, his gaze dead ahead.

Brutus, standing nearer than the rest from his exchange with the servant, sheathed his bloody blade and raised his hands in greeting. "Welcome, Mark Antony!"

But Antony did not respond. He strode past Brutus, past the other conspirators, until he stood, as unmoving as a statue, before the bloody body of Julius Caesar.

The conspirators exchanged wary glances. Cassius gripped his sword tighter than ever, and even Brutus felt misgivings rising in his gut. The tension held ...

... until, finally, Antony spoke.

"Oh, mighty Caesar! Do you lie so low? Are all your conquests, glories, triumphs, spoils, shrunk to *this* little measure? Farewell."

Antony closed his eyes a moment, then he straightened his shoulders and looked to the men around him, Brutus in particular.

"I do not know, gentlemen," he said, "what you intend, who else 'must' bleed, who else is 'corrupt.' If *I* myself, there is no hour so fitting as *Caesar's* death's hour, nor no instrument of half that worth as those, your swords – made rich with the most noble blood of all this world. I do beg you, if you bear a grudge against me ... *now*, while your purpled hands do reek and smoke, fulfill your pleasure. If I live a thousand years, I shall not find myself so ready to die; no place will please me so, no means of death, as here – beside Caesar – and cut off by you, the choice and master spirits of this new age."

Brutus shook his head with vehemence. "Oh, Antony, do not beg your death of us! Though now we must appear bloody and cruel – as by our hands and this, our present act, you see we do – yet you see *only* our hands, and this, the bleeding business they have done. Our *hearts* you do not see; they are full of pity for Caesar ... but pity to the general wrong of Rome – as fire drives out fire, so pity drives out pity – has done this deed on Caesar." He spread his bloody hands. "For your part, to you, our swords have soft points, Mark Antony. Our arms, with the same strength as performed this act, and our hearts, full of brothers' temper, do receive you with all kind love, good thoughts, and reverence."

Before Antony could respond or Brutus could speak further, Cassius cut in. "Your voice," he said to Antony, "shall be as strong as any man's in the distributing of new offices."

Brutus glanced at Cassius, but added to Antony, "Only be patient till we have appeased the multitude, who are beside themselves with fear, and then we will deliver to you the cause why I – that did love Caesar when I struck him – have proceeded in this manner."

Antony considered this for several long seconds. Then he spoke, "I do not doubt your wisdom. Let each man render me his bloody hand. First, Marcus Brutus, I will shake with you." And he stepped forward to do just that, extending his hand.

Brutus offered a thoughtful smile as he accepted Antony's grasp.

The others exchanged surprised, awkward looks; though Cassius had been the most suspicious of Mark Antony, none of them had expected this encounter to proceed in such smooth fashion. As one, they began tucking away their blades.

"Next," Antony said, "Caius Cassius, I do take your hand."

Cassius had held onto his sword the longest, but in spite of the uncertainty on his face, he, too, accepted Antony's hand.

Antony moved down the line of them. "Now, Decius Brutus,

yours ... now yours, Metellus ... yours, Cinna ... and, my valiant Casca, yours ... though last, not least in love, yours, good Trebonius."

When the exchanges were complete, Antony peered down at his own hand, now quite bloody itself. He drifted back to Caesar's body as he considered that sanguine stain, then sighed and faced them once more.

"Gentlemen all – alas! What shall I say?" He held up his bloody hand for their inspection. "My credit now stands on such slippery ground that one of two bad ways you must judge me – either a coward or a flatterer."

Antony lowered his hand and looked down, addressing his deceased friend.

"That I did love you, Caesar, oh, it is true; if then your spirit looks upon us now, shall it not grieve you more keenly than your death to see your Antony making his peace, shaking the bloody fingers of your foes – most noble – in the presence of your corpse? Had I as many eyes as you have wounds, weeping as fast as they stream forth your blood, it would become me better than to unite in terms of 'friendship' with your *enemies* ..."

Cassius looked to Brutus: Did Brutus not hear these words? Did this speech not prove Antony dangerous, not to be trusted?

Antony continued, "Pardon me, Julius! Here you were brought down like a stag, you brave hart ... here you did fall ... and here your hunters stand, marked and crimsoned in your stream of death." He shook his head. "Oh world, you were the forest to this hart, and this indeed, oh world, the heart of *you*. How like a deer, struck by many 'princes,' you do lie here!"

Cassius could listen no further. If Brutus would not speak, would not make challenge, then he would. He stepped forward, beginning, "Mark Antony—"

Antony snapped his head up, his eyes ablaze, and barked, "*Pardon me*, Caius Cassius!"

Cassius stopped short, his hand yearning to draw forth his sword once more.

But then Antony blinked and the flame within seemed to cool. He offered the slightest smile and explained, "Even the enemies of Caesar shall say all this; then – in a friend – it is cold moderation."

Cassius was not convinced. "I do not blame you for praising Caesar so, but what compact do you mean to have with *us?* Will you be marked on the list of our 'friends' ... or shall we move on, and not depend on you?"

Antony retorted, "That is why I took your hands, but was indeed swayed from the point by looking down on Caesar. I am friends with you all, and love you all, upon this hope: That you shall give me *reasons* why, and in what respect, Caesar was dangerous."

Brutus expressed his wholehearted agreement, "Or else this was a savage spectacle. Our reasons are so full of good consideration that were you, Antony, the *son* of Caesar, you should be satisfied."

"That's all I seek," Antony replied, "and am, moreover, petitioner that I may produce his body to the marketplace, and in the pulpit – as becomes a friend – speak in the ceremony of his funeral."

Brutus declared with ease, "You shall, Mark Antony."

Cassius had already begun shaking his head in denial when Brutus said this. Struggling to keep his expression neutral, he placed his hand on Brutus' shoulder. "Brutus, a word with you."

Brutus appeared somewhat taken aback – which further frustrated Cassius – but he nodded and allowed himself to be led away from Antony and the others, leaving them all to stare at one another with leery eyes as they awaited the men's return.

When they had achieved some distance, Cassius assailed Brutus with a furious whisper, "You do not know what you do! Do not consent that Antony speak in his funeral. Do you know how much the people may be moved by that which he will utter?"

But Brutus offered a placative shake of his head. "By your pardon," he whispered in a much calmer voice, "I will myself go into the pulpit *first,* and show the reason of our Caesar's death. What Antony shall speak, I will proclaim he speaks by our leave and by our permission, and that we are contented Caesar shall have all true rites and lawful ceremonies. It shall advantage more than do us wrong."

Cassius remained unconvinced. "I do not know what may happen," he said through gritted teeth. "I do not like it." He turned his back on Brutus and paced away.

Brutus saw that their heated exchange had not escaped the notice of either their fellow conspirators or Mark Antony, but there was nothing for it.

Returning to the group, Brutus stated, "Mark Antony, here, take Caesar's body." But after Antony nodded his thanks, Brutus put greater steel into his voice. "You shall *not*, in your funeral speech, blame us, but speak all good you can devise of Caesar, and say you do it by our permission; or else, you shall not have any hand at all about his funeral. And you shall speak in the same pulpit to which I am going – *after* my speech is ended."

Antony nodded again, this time in assent. "It shall be so. I do desire no more."

Brutus smiled in satisfaction. "Prepare the body, then, and follow us." He gestured for his fellows to accompany him, and so they did – even, in spite of his brooding, Cassius – as he led them out of the Senate-House.

Antony watched them go, listened as the cries of the crowds greeted them, stood rigid as they disappeared from view – all save Brutus, who offered one last, long look back at Antony and dead Caesar, before finally closing the great doors behind him.

Once the echoes of those doors faded throughout the great hall, Antony released his tight breath, and the fist he had kept low at his side, clenched so that his nails had threatened to break through the flesh of his palm. He knelt by the body of his dear, lost friend, his eyes glistening with embittered tears of sorrow, and of rage.

"Oh, pardon me," he hissed through strained lips, "you bleeding piece of earth, that I am meek and gentle with these butchers! You are the ruins of the noblest man that ever lived in the ebb and flow of history. Woe to the hand that shed this precious blood! Over your wounds – which, like dumb mouths, do open their ruby lips to beg the voice and utterance of my tongue – do I now prophesy: A curse shall light upon the limbs of men; domestic fury and fierce civil strife shall cumber all the parts of Italy; blood and destruction shall be so common and dreadful sights so familiar, that mothers shall simply smile when they behold their infants torn apart with the hands of war; all pity choked with the frequency of cruel deeds ..." Unable to help himself, discretion be damned, Antony rose to his feet as his voice rose in volume. "... and *Caesar's spirit*, seeking revenge, with Ate, Greek goddess of discord, by his side come hot from hell, shall in these regions with a monarch's voice cry *'Havoc!'* and let slip the dogs of war; that *this foul deed* shall smell above the earth with carrion men, groaning for burial."

The Senate-House door creaked open just far enough to allow entrance for one slender man. The fellow spied Antony and, after a heartbeat of hesitation, made his way toward him.

As the man drew nearer, Antony recognized him from his visitations with Julius Caesar's great-nephew. "You serve Octavius Caesar, do you not?"

The slender servant halted and bowed. "I do, Mark Antony."

"Caesar did write for him to come to Rome."

The servant nodded. "He did receive his letters, and is coming, and bid me say to you by word of mouth—" The servant froze when he absorbed who it was lying at Antony's feet. He gasped, "Oh, Caesar!"

"Your heart is big," Antony said. "Allow yourself to weep. Passion, I see, is catching, for my eyes – seeing those beads of sorrow standing in yours – began to water. Is your master coming?"

Collecting himself as best he could, the slender servant answered, "He lies tonight within seven leagues of Rome."

Antony nodded his satisfaction. "Post back with speed and tell him what has occurred. Here is a mourning Rome, a *dangerous* Rome, no Rome of safety for Octavius yet; hurry forth and tell him so."

The servant bowed and made to do just that, but Antony forestalled him with a gesture.

"Yet, stay awhile," he said. "You shall not go back till I have borne this corpse into the marketplace. There I shall test, in my oration, how the people take the cruel deed of these bloody men – according to the outcome, you shall discourse to young Octavius of the state of things."

The servant nodded his understanding.

They stood still a while longer, each of them staring upon noble Caesar.

At last, Antony ordered, "Lend me your hand."

And together, they knelt beside the cooling body.

PART THREE

CHAPTER TWO

The riotous crowd surrounding the Roman Forum stewed in a simmering mass, a cacophony of cries, curses, tears, and animosity that threatened to deafen all of Italy.

Cassius spoke with urgency near Brutus' ear, but Brutus only caught bits and pieces of it; it sounded as though the man were already trying to designate their hold over the late Julius Caesar's plunder – Brutus should govern Macedonia; he, Cassius, should control Syria; Decius should rule Cisalpine Gaul, and so on. While Brutus agreed that wise guiding hands would be required to control the void left by Caesar's death – only, of course, until the Senate could rebound into its proper place – he found it irritating that Cassius could not see that this was neither the time nor place nor circumstances to discuss such matters.

Then the citizens of Rome saw the conspirators approaching the pulpit, and their focus shifted like a wrathful tide.

Without hesitation, Brutus held his arms high; one hand grasping his bloodied dagger, the other itself smeared with Caesar's blood. His confederates followed his lead.

A tense hush fell upon the crowd; they had not expected such bold, brazen behavior. Only a few among the plebeians found voices with which to speak, demanding an understanding of the affairs which had taken place in the Capitol: "We will be satisfied!" cried one. "Let us be satisfied!" cried another.

Brutus returned in a commanding, yet calm, voice, "Then follow me, and give me audience, friends."

This was greeted by throbbing murmurs, but at least they did not return to screaming. Not yet.

"Cassius," Brutus said, his voice still raised, "you go into the other street and part the numbers." Cassius did not appear pleased by this, but Brutus continued, louder, "Those that will hear me speak, let them stay here; those that will follow Cassius, go with him; and public reasons shall be rendered of Caesar's death."

The throng seemed somewhat mollified by this promise. Brutus caught snatches of their words: "I will hear Brutus speak" and "I will hear Cassius, and compare their reasons when, separately, we hear them rendered" and so on.

Casting a final, uncertain look to Brutus, Cassius raised his grisly sword higher and departed, followed by a fair portion of the expectant crowd, but most of them remained. Brutus nodded to the other conspirators, then climbed the stairs to the pulpit.

"The noble Brutus is ascended!" declared another plebeian. "Silence!"

Brutus sheathed his dagger, then held his bloody hands over his head again. As the crowd began to grumble anew, he called, "Be patient till the last."

The masses hushed once more, as best any such collection of bodies could.

Lowering his arms so that Caesar's blood fell from sight, Brutus began in earnest.

"Romans, countrymen, and friends, *hear* me for my cause, and be silent that you may hear. *Believe* me for my honor, and bear my honor in mind that you may believe. *Judge* me in your wisdom, and awake your senses that you may the better judge." He paused a single breath, then proclaimed, "If there are any in this assembly, any dear friend of Caesar's, to him I say that *Brutus'* love for Caesar was no less than his. If then that friend demands why Brutus rose against Caesar, this is my answer: *Not* that I loved Caesar less, but that I loved *Rome* more!"

The crowd shuffled, exchanging looks with one another, but no one challenged Brutus' words.

"Would you rather Caesar were living, and die all *slaves*, than that Caesar were dead, to live all *free men*?"

This time the crowd rumbled a bit, their collective words summed as a denial to this supposed loss of their freedom.

"As Caesar loved me," Brutus continued, "I weep for him; as he was fortunate, I rejoice at it; as he was valiant, I honor him ... but, as he was *ambitious*, I *slew* him! There are tears for his love; joy for his fortune; honor for his valor ... and *death* for his *ambition*." He cast his gaze about the crowd. "Who is here so lowly that would be a slave? If any, speak, for *him* have I offended. Who is here so uncivilized that would not be a Roman? If any, speak, for *him* have I offended. Who is here so vile that will not love his country? If any, speak, for *him* have I offended." Brutus clasped his hands before him, exuding a patient demeanor. "I pause for a reply."

So silent had the crowd fallen that, for a long moment, Brutus thought perhaps he would receive no reply of any kind. But at last, a male voice called out, and his words were echoed across the masses: "None, Brutus, none!"

Brutus nodded. "Then *none* have I offended. I have done no more to Caesar than *you* shall do to *Brutus*. The justification for his death is recorded in the Capitol – his glory not belittled wherein he was worthy, nor his offenses unduly stressed for which he suffered death."

Then a wave of rekindled agitation thrummed through the crowd, ushered by muffled cries and gasps. Within seconds, Brutus determined the cause: Mark Antony had arrived; together with an unfamiliar manservant, he bore the body of Caesar, the late *Dictator Perpetuo's* cloak wrapped to enshroud his face and his gory wounds.

Determined to maintain control, Brutus gestured toward Antony so that none could miss him. "Here comes his body," he called, "mourned by Mark Antony, who, though he had *no hand* in Caesar's death, shall receive the benefit of his dying – a share in the commonwealth; as which of you shall not?"

Antony led the servant to the landing below the pulpit and, taking the full weight of their sad burden into his own arms as the servant slipped away, he laid down the departed Caesar. A fair amount of Caesar's blood had soaked through the cloak surrounding his body, and when Antony stood erect and silent, blood was visible upon him as well.

Not wishing the plebeians to ponder this sight too long, Brutus announced, "With this I depart: That, as I slew my best friend for the good of Rome ..." He reached into his robes and brandished his blade high above his head. "... I have the same dagger *for myself*, when it shall please my country to need *my* death."

"Live, Brutus," cried the masses, "live, live!"

Brutus lowered his dagger and sheathed it; amongst the crowd, his fellow conspirators exchanged satisfied looks.

Mark Antony did nothing, said nothing, but stood stolid and motionless, staring out at the horde that had shifted from mourning Caesar to cheering the very man who helped murder his dear friend.

The Roman citizens continued their enthusiastic embracement of Brutus.

"Bring him, with triumph, home to his house!"

"Give him a statue with his ancestors!"

"Let *him* be Caesar!"

"Caesar's better parts shall be crowned in Brutus!"

"We'll bring him to his house with shouts and clamors!"

At last, Brutus held his arms aloft again, trying to be heard over them. "My countrymen—!"

"Peace, silence!" someone called. "Brutus speaks!"

The words were echoed, "Peace, ho!"

When the clamoring finally lowered to a manageable level, Brutus declared, "Good countrymen, let me depart alone, and, for my sake, stay here with Antony. Pay respect to Caesar's corpse, and grace his speech tending to Caesar's glories, which Mark Antony – by our permission – is allowed to make. I do entreat you: Not a man depart, save I alone, till Antony has spoken."

With that, Brutus nodded to Antony – who returned the gesture with the barest minimum of movement – then he exited the pulpit, his head held high and his eyes only forward, as he made his way through the crowd and away from the Forum.

Some of the citizens, fully satisfied by what they had heard from Brutus, began ambling away as well. But a few voices protested: "Stay, ho, and let us hear Mark Antony!"

One citizen in particular, who stood near to Antony and Caesar's body, called, "Let him go up into the public chair; we'll hear him!" He then said directly to Antony, "Noble Antony, go up."

Antony met this with apparent indifference, almost shrugging as he replied, "For Brutus' sake, I am beholden to you." With that, he turned and – with slow, deliberate strides – climbed the steps toward the pulpit.

One citizen asked, "What does he say of Brutus?"

"He says for Brutus' sake," another replied, "he finds himself beholden to us all."

The first citizen scowled. "It were best he speak no harm of Brutus here."

Many heads nodded, and many voices chimed in.

"This Caesar was a tyrant."

"Nay, that's certain. We are blessed that Rome is rid of him."

"Peace," one called over the others, "let us hear what Antony can say."

Antony, who had reached the pulpit, looked down upon his dead friend, then began to address the disinterested crowd. "You gentle Romans—"

"Peace, ho!" called out more of the citizens. "Let us hear him!"

At last, the skeptical citizens settled enough to allow Antony to speak.

"Friends ..." he called anew in a stronger voice, "Romans ... countrymen ... lend me your ears! I come to bury Caesar, not to praise him."

Many heads nodded in affirmation of this declaration. A proper burial was appropriate – so long as Antony did not try to dissuade them from Brutus' noble words, most of them were inclined to listen further.

"The evil that men do lives after them," Antony continued, "the good is often interred with their bones; so let it be with Caesar. The noble Brutus has told you Caesar was 'ambitious' – if it were so, it was a grievous fault, and grievously has Caesar atoned for it. Here, under leave of Brutus and the rest – for Brutus is an *honorable* man; so are they all, all *honorable* men – I come to speak in Caesar's funeral."

This was greeted with more nods. Antony, calling Brutus honorable, spoke fair and true, and there was no further shuffling toward the side streets away from the Forum.

"Caesar was my friend," said Antony, "faithful and just to me ...

but Brutus says he was 'ambitious,' and Brutus is an *honorable* man."
But then Antony appeared thoughtful, and he gestured down to
Caesar. "He has brought many captives home to Rome, whose
ransoms did fill the public treasury; did this, in Caesar, seem
'ambitious'? When the poor have cried, Caesar has wept; 'ambition'
should be made of sterner stuff! Yet Brutus says he was 'ambitious,'
and Brutus is an *honorable* man."

The crowd began to shift and shuffle once more, but no longer
in skepticism or resistance; Antony's words had them exchanging
uncertain glances and wringing their hands.

Antony swept his arm out over the citizens before him. "You all
did see that, on the Feast of Lupercal, I *thrice* presented him a kingly
crown, which he did thrice *refuse*. Was *this* 'ambition'? Yet Brutus
says he was 'ambitious;' and, sure, he is an *honorable* man!"

The citizens greeted this with more uncertain looks, more wrung
hands, and a release of confused tears from more than one pair of
eyes.

This budding reversal in the crowd's temperament unnerved
Brutus' confederates, and they began slipping away, withdrawing
from the scene with as gentle a step as they could manage.

"I do not speak to disprove what Brutus spoke," Antony assured
the assembly, "but here I am to speak what I do know: You all did
love him once, not without cause. What cause withholds you, then, to
mourn for him?" And at this, Antony seemed to lose control of
himself, his next words flowing forth with great ire. "Oh judgment,
you have fled to brutish beasts, and *men* have lost their reason!"

A few citizens nearest to the pulpit actually retreated a step from
this sudden wrath and bitterness. But then Antony shook his head and
waved his hands as if struggling to regain control of himself.

"Bear with me ..." he pleaded in a broken voice, "... my heart is
'in the coffin' there with Caesar ... and I must pause till it comes back
to me." Covering his face as though unable to withhold his tears any
longer, Antony turned away from the crowd.

The atmosphere in the Forum had grown oppressive. None
among them wanted to disturb Mark Antony during his moment of
vulnerability, but his words had already roused them from the
satisfaction given by Marcus Brutus.

At last, one plebeian voiced her renewed doubts. "I think there is much reason in his sayings."

Another agreed, "If you consider rightly of the matter, Caesar has had great wrong."

"Has he, masters? I fear someone worse will come in his place."

"Did you mark his words? Caesar would not take the crown; therefore it is certain he was *not* ambitious."

"If it is found so, some will pay dearly for it."

When Antony turned around to face the masses once more, he gasped a few more breaths, as though still not quite ready to proceed.

"Poor soul, his eyes are red as fire with weeping."

"There's not a nobler man in Rome than Antony."

At last, one called out over the others, "Now mark him, he begins again to speak!"

Indeed, Antony had raised a hand, and all among them fell silent.

"Just yesterday," he continued, "the word of Caesar might have stood against the world; now he lies there, and none are so humble as to revere him." He offered a disgusted shake of his head as he looked out over the crowd. "Oh masters, if I were disposed to stir your hearts and minds to mutiny and rage, I should do Brutus wrong, and Cassius wrong, who – you all know – are 'honorable' men." He shook his head again. "I will not do them wrong; I would rather choose to wrong the dead, to wrong myself, and you, than I will wrong such 'honorable' men." Then he reached into his robes and produced something which he held aloft for all to see. "But here's a parchment with the seal of Caesar; I found it in his study – it is his *will!*"

A few in the crowd gasped at this, but most remained silent and rapt.

Antony considered the sealed parchment as though surprised to find it in his hand ... and then he returned it to his robes, which caused a greater stir than when he identified it. And as he spoke, the fire returned to his voice. "Allow the common people to hear this testament – which, pardon me, I do not mean to read – and they would go and kiss dead Caesar's wounds, and dip their handkerchiefs in his sacred blood; yea, beg a hair from him for memory and, dying, mention it within *their* wills, bequeathing it as a rich legacy unto their heirs!"

"We'll hear the will!" someone called. "Read it, Mark Antony!"

"The will, the will!" echoed other voices in increasing numbers. "We will hear Caesar's will!"

But Antony called out, "Have patience, gentle friends; I must *not* read it. It is not appropriate for you to know how Caesar loved you – you are not wood, you are not stones, but *men*. And, being men, hearing the will of Caesar, it will *inflame* you, it will make you *mad*! It is good you not know that *you* are his heirs, for if you should – oh, what would come of it?"

"Read the will!" a man in front demanded. "We'll hear it, Antony!"

Others cried, "You shall read us the will, Caesar's will!"

Still Antony denied them. "Will you be patient? Will you wait awhile? I have overshot myself to tell you of it. I fear I wrong the 'honorable' men whose daggers have stabbed Caesar; I do fear it!"

"They were traitors!" someone screamed. " 'Honorable' men?!"

"The will! The testament!"

"They were villains, murderers! The will! Read the will!"

Antony approached the very edge of the pulpit, looming over the body below, the body of dear, murdered Caesar. "You will compel me, then, to read the will?" And when the crowd called its confirmation, he pointed downward. "Then make a ring about the corpse of Caesar, and let me show you him that *made* the will." He took one step to exit the pulpit, then stopped and asked, in a humble voice, "Shall I descend? And will you give me leave?"

"Come down!"

"Descend!"

"You shall have leave!"

And with that, Antony descended from the pulpit.

"A ring," one citizen commanded the others, "stand round!"

"Stand from the hearse," another citizen insisted, indicating the platform beneath the pulpit, "stand from the body!"

"Room for Antony," cried a third, "most noble Antony!"

When Antony returned to late Caesar, the crowd still pushed forward, and he stated, "Nay, do not press so upon me. Stand far off."

"Stand back!" the plebeians urged one another. "Room! Bear

back!"

After another pregnant pause, Antony at last said, "If you have tears, prepare to shed them now." He knelt next to Caesar, his hand sweeping across the stained cloak which covered most of the body from sight. "You all do know this mantle. I remember the first time ever Caesar put it on. It was on a summer's evening in his tent, that day he overcame the Nervii – that fierce Gallic tribe, descended from the Gauls, who sacked Rome centuries ago."

As the heads nearest to him nodded in memory of Caesar's magnificent conquest, Antony ran his hands over the cloak until it found a notable hole. He fingered the jagged, bloody breach. "Look, in this place Cassius' dagger ran through." He found another hole. "See what a rent the malicious Casca made." He sought yet another hole, and this one he drove his fingers through to seize it, his hand shaking in anger. "Through this the well-beloved Brutus stabbed, and, as he plucked his cursed steel away, note how the blood of Caesar followed it, as though rushing out of doors to make certain whether or not it was *Brutus* who so cruelly knocked – for Brutus, as you know, was Caesar's angel." He raised his face to the heavens. "Judge, oh you gods, how dearly Caesar loved him!" He shook the cloak where his fingers gripped Brutus' alleged point of attack. "*This* was the most unkindest cut of all! For when the noble Caesar saw *Brutus* stab, ingratitude – more strong than traitors' arms – quite vanquished him! Then his mighty heart burst; and, in his cloak muffling up his face, even at the base of Pompey's statue – which, all the while, ran blood – great ... Caesar ... *fell*." He shook his head as though in denial. "Oh, what a fall was there, my countrymen! Then I and you and all of us fell down, while bloody treason flourished over us!"

Releasing Caesar's cloak, Antony rose back to his feet, and many of the eyes which followed were indeed shedding tears.

"Oh," Antony commented, "now you weep, and I perceive you feel the impression of pity. These are gracious drops. Kind souls, what, you weep when you only behold our Caesar's *clothes* wounded? Look you here ..."

To the shock of all, Antony reached down and ripped away the cloak, exposing Caesar's mutilated body for everyone to see.

"... here is himself," he called out, "marred, as you see, by *traitors*!"

At the sight of the many wounds inflicted upon Caesar's gory remains, the crowd was struck dumb, and silence fell across the Forum for several long seconds.

Then one citizen cried, "Oh, piteous spectacle!"

Another choked, "Oh, noble Caesar!"

Then more joined in as Antony watched, and waited.

"Oh, woeful day!"

"Oh traitors, villains!"

"Oh, most bloody sight!"

"We will be revenged!"

Soon the words washed over each other, mixing into a tumult of indignation, injustice, and rage.

"Revenge!"

"Go about!"

"Seek!"

"Burn!"

"Fire!"

"Kill!"

"Slay!"

"*Let not a traitor live*!"

The crowd began to surge forth from the Forum, but Antony called out in his loudest voice, "Stay, countrymen!"

"Peace there!" shouted one citizen. "Hear the noble Antony!"

"We'll hear him," another plebeian echoed, "we'll follow him, we'll *die* with him!"

Once they had calmed enough to listen further, Antony offered them an approximation of a smile. "Good friends, sweet friends, do not let me stir you up to such a sudden flood of mutiny. They that have done this deed are 'honorable.' What private grievances they have, alas, I do not know what made them do it. They are wise ... and 'honorable' ... and will, no doubt, answer you with *reasons*."

Antony shook his head and released a heavy sigh.

"I do not come, friends, to steal away your hearts. I am no orator, as Brutus is; but, as you all know me, a plain blunt man, that loved my friend; and those who gave me public leave to speak of him know that full well. For I have neither wit, nor words, nor worth, nor the good gestures of strong delivery, nor the power of speech to stir men's blood – I only speak with humble *honesty*. I tell you that which you yourselves do know, show you sweet Caesar's wounds – poor, poor mute mouths – and bid them speak *for* me."

Antony shook his head again, but no heavy sigh this time – no, this time his jaws clenched so that the muscles flexed and spasmed, and his next words built in volume and righteous fury.

"But if *I* were Brutus ... and if *Brutus* were Antony ... *there* would be an Antony who would ruffle up your spirits, and put a tongue in *every wound* of Caesar, that should move the *stones* of Rome to *rise and mutiny*!"

The crowd burst forth with cries of, "We'll mutiny!"

One man followed, "We'll burn the house of Brutus!"

Another began shoving those around him. "Away then! Come, seek the conspirators!"

But once more, Antony reined them back. "Yet hear me, countrymen, yet hear me speak!"

"Peace, ho!" the crowd chided one another. "Hear Antony, most noble Antony!"

When the masses had settled once again, Antony declared, "Why, friends, you do not know what you go to do! In what way has Caesar so deserved your loves? Alas, you do not know! I must tell you then: You have forgot the *will* I told you of!"

"Most true!" they cried.

"The will!"

"Let's stay and hear the will!"

As they shouted and called and clamored, Antony made his way back to the pulpit. Upon reaching it, he thrust his hand into his robes and produced the parchment with great flourish for all to see.

"Here is the will," Antony called, "and under Caesar's seal!" He then broke the seal in front of the many witnesses, unrolled the parchment, and read it to them. "To every Roman citizen he gives – to *every individual* man – seventy-five drachmas!"

The plebeians gasped. Seventy-five of the silver Greek coins would be a sweet boon to some, and a boost in the quality of life for others.

"Most noble Caesar!" a man cried. "We'll revenge his death!"

"Oh, royal Caesar!"

And still, Antony waved them down. "Hear me with patience!"

"Peace, ho!" they subdued one another.

"Moreover," Antony continued reading the parchment, "he has left you all his walks, his private arbors, and new-planted orchards, on this side of the river Tiber; he has left them to you, and to your heirs forever – common pleasure-grounds in which to walk abroad and enjoy yourselves."

Antony lowered the parchment, and pointed down to the body of his dead friend.

"*Here* was a *Caesar*!" he roared. "*When* comes such *another*?!"

Inflamed by Antony's words, one of the citizens cried, "Never, *never*!" The man then moved forward to stand over Caesar's body as he turned to face the crowd. "Come, away, away! We'll burn Caesar's body in the holy place, and with the brands, set fire to the traitors' houses! Take up the body!"

Another joined in, "Go fetch fire!"

A third, "Pluck down benches!"

A forth, "Pluck down benches, shutters, anything!"

And with that, the masses would be bridled no longer. They surged to and fro, some collecting Caesar's remains, others calling for the conspirators' heads, others still doing nothing more than screaming, thrashing about, causing as much damage to the Forum at large as they intended to do to the traitors.

They had become a heedless, writhing, seething organism of rage and revenge.

Just as Mark Antony intended.

Gazing upon his work, Antony felt a satisfied smile gracing his lips. *Now let it work. Mischief, you are afoot; take whatever course you wish!*

Movement at his side drew his attention from the chaos before him, and he saw that Octavius Caesar's servant had returned. "What now, fellow?"

The servant, his eyes widened by the pandemonium below, bowed to Antony. "Sir, Octavius has already come to Rome."

"Where is he?"

"He and Lepidus are at Caesar's house."

Antony stated, "And there I will go at once to visit him." Then he chuckled to himself, "He comes as if upon my wish."

In truth, Octavius – here, now, after all – posed a potential complication for Antony: He had read aloud only the portions of Caesar's will that suited him; what he had withheld was the fact that Julius Caesar had also named Octavius as his one true heir, posthumously adopting him as his own son – solidifying the "Caesar" of Octavius' name.

But this did not truly concern Antony; he had handled the crowd, and he would handle young Octavius.

When he saw some confusion on the servant's face over his last words, he smiled again. "Fortune is merry, and in this mood will give us anything."

The servant nodded his understanding. "I heard him say Brutus and Cassius have ridden like madmen through the gates of Rome."

Antony offered an open laugh to that and gestured to the riot taking place. "Likely they had some notice of the people, how I had moved them." He sighed in pleasure at his good work, then clapped his hand upon the servant's shoulder. "Bring me to Octavius."

And with that, they took their leave of the sheer madness that had seized the Roman Forum.

PART THREE

CHAPTER THREE

The poet known as Cinna made his way through the chaotic streets of Rome. The raucous citizens running past gave him pause, particularly the torches they waved about in such a manner that suggested far more aggression than simply "lighting their way." Under other circumstances, he would have returned to his humble domicile and waited out this turmoil, but word had spread that poor, late Julius Caesar's body was to be burned in the holy place, and ...

I dreamt last night, Cinna the poet thought, *that I did feast with Caesar, and things filled my fantasy with ominous forebodings.*

I have no will to wander forth of doors, yet something leads me forth.

And so, he continued along his way, trying to remain as inconspicuous as possible.

But when the latest band of plebeians wandered past, his efforts failed; one of the men took note of him and stopped, and the others followed his lead.

"What is your name?" the man demanded.

Before the poet could respond, another snapped, "Where are you going?"

A third, an older man with shaggy grey hair, peered at him with a disconcerting gleam in his torch-lit eyes. "Where do you dwell?"

"Are you a married man," barked a fourth man, "or a bachelor?"

The poet stared from one to the other, overwhelmed by their vehemence, and his delay in replying further agitated his inquisitors.

"Answer every man directly."

"Aye, and briefly."

"Aye, and wisely."

"Aye," added the shaggy man with a dark grin, "and *truly* would be best for you."

After a nervous swallow, Cinna the poet at last found his words again.

"What is my name?" he repeated. "Where am I going? Where do I dwell? Am I a married man or a bachelor?" When the group responded with greedy nods, he continued, "Then to answer every man directly and briefly, wisely and truly: Wisely I say, I am a bachelor."

"That," the second man interrupted, "is as much as to say that they are fools that do marry. You'll suffer a blow from me for that, I fear." The poet shook his head, denying that this was his intention, but the second man snapped his fingers in impatience — overlooking his own interference in the poet's answering. "Proceed directly!"

The poet licked his lips and continued, "Directly, I am going to Caesar's funeral."

The first man seized his arm. "As a friend or an enemy?"

"As a friend," the poet assured him.

The second man chimed in, "*That* matter is answered directly."

The fourth man sneered, "Now for your dwelling – briefly!"

The poet, with a careful touch, removed the hand from his arm. "Briefly, I dwell by the Capitol."

The shaggy man loomed over him. "Your *name*, sir, truly."

The poet replied, "Truly, my name is Cinna."

The response was immediate and violent. The poet was seized again, this time by both arms, and shoved against the nearest wall; his head struck the stone and stars flashed before his eyes.

"Tear him to pieces!" the first man roared. "He's a conspirator!"

The poet shook his head. "I am Cinna the *poet*," he wheezed, "I am Cinna the *poet*!"

"Tear him for his bad verses," the fourth man laughed, "tear him for his bad verses!"

Cinna the poet shook his head again, a wild shoulder-to-shoulder gesture which caused more pain to shoot down his neck, but he was desperate to reason with them. He pleaded, "I am *not* Cinna the conspirator!"

The fourth man spat to the others, "It is no matter, his name's

'Cinna'! Pluck nothing but his *name* out of his heart and dispatch him!"

The shaggy man screamed in dark joy, "Tear him apart, tear him apart!" And as his partners in crime proceeded to do just that, he turned and called to all the fellow rioters within earshot.

"Come, firebrands, ho!" he cried at the top of his lungs. "Firebrands! To Brutus' house, to Cassius', burn all! Some to Decius' house, and some to Casca's, some to Ligarius'." He thrust his arms into the air in imagined victory. "Away, go!"

And so the rioters stormed off to their next errand of brutality and destruction, dragging what remained of Cinna the poet along with them.

PART FOUR

CHAPTER ONE

Rioting throughout the great city eventually settled. The initial shock of Caesar's death faded, and all the tangible fallout and political intrigue within the Roman Empire were, if not fully resolved, at least somewhat stabilized.

After all that, the new central power of Rome – Mark Antony, Octavius Caesar, and Marcus Aemilius Lepidus, the Roman general who joined with Octavius on the outskirts of Rome on the day of Julius Caesar's assassination – chose to model themselves after the structure established by Julius Caesar, Pompey, and Crassus. Indeed, they openly embraced the label of "the Second Triumvirate."

Soon thereafter, Antony informed his fellow Triumvirs that it was time they discussed certain matters that were best ratified away from the prying eyes and curious ears of the Capitol. Octavius agreed, and therefore, so did Lepidus.

And so, one evening as the sun set over Rome, this Second Triumvirate gathered at Antony's house. After sharing a modest meal, the three remained at the table, drawing up long lists of names – though, to Lepidus' eye, the other men's lists seemed a degree longer than his own.

Setting aside his writing implements, Antony reviewed his papyrus. He then declared, "These many, then, shall die; their names are marked."

Octavius, inspecting his own list, agreed with a nod. Then he looked to Lepidus. "Your brother, too, must die. Do you consent, Lepidus?"

Lepidus hesitated, then said, "I do consent ..."

Octavius nodded again and said, "Mark him down, Antony."

But Lepidus was not finished. "... upon condition: *Publius* – who is your sister's son, Mark Antony – shall not live."

Antony answered with a casual shrug. "He shall not live; look, with a mark I damn him." Antony struck his nephew's name upon the list and pushed the papyrus aside. He then considered all that Caesar had bequeathed to the many citizens of Rome. "But, Lepidus, go to Caesar's house; fetch the will here, and we shall determine how to reduce some expenditures in his legacies."

Lepidus appeared disgruntled at being assigned such a menial task. But a glance informed him that he would receive no support from Octavius, so he swallowed his pride and stood. "What, shall I find you here?"

Octavius was back to writing and did not look up as he answered, "Here, or at the Capitol."

Lepidus nodded to them both and marched from the room. Antony heard him collect one of the waiting soldiers as a personal guard, then exit the premises.

Antony wasted no time in addressing the matter on his mind. He gestured toward the departed Lepidus and shook his head with some distaste. "This is a worthless man without merit, suitable to be sent on errands; is it fit – in the world divided threefold – *he* should stand one of the three to share it?"

Octavius looked up at him in mild surprise. "So you thought him, and accepted his vote as to who should be marked to die in the black sentence of our proscription." He indicated the death lists before them, the ink still wet.

Antony kept his voice level and friendly as he said, "Octavius, I have seen more days than you; and though we lay these honors on this man to ease ourselves of diverse loads of slander, he shall only bear them as the donkey bears gold – to groan and sweat under the business, either led or driven, as *we* point the way." He leaned back in his seat. "And, having brought our treasure where we will, then we will take down his load, and turn him off – like the unladen donkey – to shake his ears and graze in public pastures."

Octavius met Antony's gaze for several long seconds. At last, he shrugged and commented. "You may do your will, but he's a tried and valiant soldier."

"So is my *horse*, Octavius," Antony said to him as though he were a naïve child, "and for that I do appoint him store of feed. It is a creature that I teach to fight, to turn, to stop, to run directly on, his corporal motion governed by *my* spirit. And, in some measure, Lepidus is nothing more: He must be taught and trained and bid go forth; a barren-spirited fellow, one that feeds on common objects, works of arts, and empty counterfeits – which, out of use and made stale by other men, then become his fashion. Do not talk of him except as a *tool*."

Octavius opened his mouth, perhaps to further protest on behalf of Lepidus, but before he could speak, Antony dismissed the entire matter.

"And now, Octavius, hear great things." He stood, his bearing far more intent. "Brutus and Cassius are levying armed forces; we must straight away raise our own army. Therefore let our alliance be strengthened, our best friends made certain, our best means extended to the utmost; and let us presently go sit in council, how covert matters may be best discovered, and open perils safely met."

Octavius stood as well. "Let us do so, for – like a captured bear, chained to a stake and at the mercy of hunting dogs – *we* are at the stake, and surrounded by many enemies. And I fear that some who smile at us have, in their hearts, millions of mischiefs."

They nodded to one another and shook hands ...

... even as, all the while, each was evaluating the other.

PART FOUR

CHAPTER TWO

The meeting of the Second Triumvirate in Rome had been a cold, calculating affair, but the gathering in Marcus Brutus' encampment was another matter altogether.

Brutus' army had marched to join Cassius' troops near Sardis, and with word that Antony and his abettors were planning to engage them soon upon the battlefield, tempers grew shorter by the day.

And Brutus anticipated Cassius' imminent arrival would be sad cause for further tension.

Upon the sounding of drums to announce the return of an envoy, Brutus emerged from his tent, accompanied by his ever-loyal boy-servant, Lucius. From the delegation, several soldiers hurried forward to greet them, including their mutual allies Lucilius and Titinius, as well as Cassius' man, Pindarus.

Eying the advancing numbers, Brutus called out, "Stand ho!"

Lucilius heard and relayed the command, "Give the word, ho, and stand!"

The troops halted their approach, giving their commanders some privacy, yet Brutus noted that the nearest stood within earshot; he considered ordering them to go about their proper business, but Lucilius, and Titinius and Pindarus awaited his acknowledgment.

"What now, Lucilius," Brutus asked, "is Cassius near?"

"He is at hand," Lucilius nodded and gestured to the man beside him, "and Pindarus has come to do you salutation from his master."

Pindarus bowed, low and with great respect.

Brutus nodded his approval of the man Cassius had sent. "He greets me well. Your master, Pindarus – in his own change of heart, or by poor officers – has given me some just cause to wish things done could be *un*done; but if he is at hand, I shall be satisfied by his explanations."

Pindarus drew back his broad shoulders. "I do not doubt that my noble master will appear such as he is – full of worthy regard and honor."

Brutus kept his expression neutral. "He is not doubted." Then he gestured off to one side. "A word, Lucilius ..."

Lucilius joined him in stepping away several strides, while Pindarus bowed again and retreated an equal distance.

Once they had achieved a semblance of privacy in this busy camp, Brutus inquired, "Let me be informed: How did Cassius receive you?"

Lucilius considered his answer. "With courtesy and with enough respect, but not with such gestures of intimacy, nor with such free and friendly conversation, as he has used of old."

Brutus sighed without surprise. "You have described a hot friendship cooling." He shook his head. "Forever note, Lucilius: When love begins to sicken and decay, it uses an enforced ceremony. There are no tricks in plain and simple faith; but insincere men – like horses fiery at the start of the race – make gallant show and promise of their mettle ... but when they should endure the bloody spur, they let their crests fall and, like deceitful, worthless nags, fail in the trial."

Brutus might have said more, but the low sound of drums and marching soldiers broke through his regretful reverie: Cassius and, by the sound, his entire military force.

He looked to Lucilius. "His army comes onward?"

"They mean to be quartered in Sardis this night," Lucilius explained. "The greater part, all his cavalry, are coming with Cassius."

As if on cue, Cassius and his primary retinue rode into sight.

"Hark," Brutus said, "he has arrived. March slowly on to meet him."

But Cassius was already calling out to his accompanying troops, "Stand ho!"

"Stand ho!" Brutus echoed. "Pass the word along."

"Stand!" called the nearest soldiers.

"Stand!"

"Stand!"

Leaving his entourage behind, Cassius leaped from his horse and advanced toward Brutus with anger clear in his eyes, his cheeks reddened and his fists clenched; hardly the behavior of a guilty man come to make his apologies to an aggrieved friend. He also appeared quite tired, and he had lost weight since Brutus last laid eyes upon him.

Cassius halted before Brutus, standing so close to him that Brutus could smell his sweat. "Most noble 'brother,' " Cassius snapped, "you have done me *wrong*."

For an instant, Brutus could only gape at Cassius' audacity. When he spoke, he grumbled, "Judge me, you gods!" To Cassius, he demanded, "Do I 'wrong' my *enemies*? And – if not so – how should I wrong a brother?"

But Cassius blundered forward, "Brutus, this sober behavior of yours hides wrongs, and when you do them—!"

With his most steely glare, Brutus cut off Cassius' rising voice, "Cassius, be calm. Speak your grievances softly; I know you well. Let us not wrangle before the eyes of both our armies here – which should perceive nothing but love between us. Bid them move away; then *in my tent*, Cassius, fully express your grievances, and I will give you audience."

Cassius made an obvious effort to rein in his indignation. After a moment, he growled to his man, who had stood nearby in awkward silence, "Pindarus, bid our commanders lead their charges off a little from this ground."

Brutus, too, ordered, "Lucilius, you do likewise, and let no man come to our tent till we have done our conference." To Cassius, he said, "Let Lucilius and Titinius guard our door."

Cassius grunted his agreement, and the two soldiers nodded their understanding.

Brutus then turned and returned to his tent, leaving Cassius to grumble further as he followed after ...

PART FOUR

CHAPTER THREE

The flaps to the tent closed but an instant before Cassius resumed his incensed assault upon Brutus.

"That you have wronged me," Cassius accused, "does appear in this: You have condemned and stigmatized Lucius Pella for 'taking bribes' here from the Sardians; whereas *my* letters – interceding on his behalf, because I knew the man – were slighted and disregarded."

Brutus met his gaze without contrition. "You wronged yourself to write in such a case."

Cassius rolled his eyes in annoyance. "In such a time as this, it is not proper that every trivial offense should be chastised."

Brutus stepped toward him, bringing them within striking distance of one another. "Let me tell you, Cassius, you yourself are often condemned for having an itching palm, for selling and marketing your offices to undeservers for gold."

Cassius ground his teeth, his jaws flexing. "*I* ... an 'itching palm'?" He made the conspicuous gesture of lifting his hand to the hilt of his sword. "You know that you are *Brutus* that speaks this, or, by the gods, this speech would be your last."

Brutus did not so much as flinch at the threat. "The name of Cassius condones this corruption, and therefore chastisement does hide its head."

"'Chastisement'?" spat Cassius.

"Remember March," Brutus cut in before he could continue, "remember the ides of March: Did great Julius not bleed for justice's sake? What villain touched his body that did not stab for justice? What, did one of us strike the foremost man of all this world only to support robbers? Shall we now contaminate our fingers with base bribes? And sell our mighty reputation for so much trash as may be grasped?" Brutus shook his head in loathing. "I would rather be a dog, and bark at the moon, than be such a Roman."

"Brutus," Cassius fumed, "do not bait me; I'll not endure it. You forget yourself to lay restrictions upon me. I am a soldier – older in experience, abler than yourself to dictate policy."

It was Brutus' turn to roll his eyes. "Nonsense! You are not, Cassius."

"I am!"

"I say you are not."

"Push me no more," Cassius warned as he gripped his sword hilt tighter still, "I shall forget myself. Have mind upon your health; tempt me no farther!"

Brutus looked at Cassius with casual contempt and made a deliberate show of turning his back. "Away, small man!"

Cassius gasped as though struck, even stepping back. He stammered, "Is it possible?"

Brutus faced Cassius once more, and in a low, overly-patient voice, he stated, "Hear me, for I will speak. Must I give way and room to your sudden anger? Shall I be frightened when a madman stares?"

Cassius' face reddened further, but he removed his hand from his weapon as he now turned away. "Oh, you gods, you gods ... must I endure all this?"

Brutus smirked. " 'All this'? Aye, more. Fret till your proud heart breaks. Go show your slaves how choleric you are and make your bondmen tremble. Must *I* flinch? Must *I* defer to you? Must *I* stand and crouch under your testy humor?"

Cassius looked back to him, opening his mouth to speak, but Brutus shook his head and continued.

"By the gods, you shall swallow the venom of your temper even if it splits you apart. For, from this day forth, I'll use you for my mirth – yea, for my laughter – when you are waspish."

Cassius sputtered, then deflated as he moved to the nearest bench and perched upon it. When he finally spoke, his tone reeked of resentment, but also of regret. "Has it come to this?"

Brutus remained standing, looking down upon him. "You say

you are a better soldier: Let it appear so; make your boasting true, and it shall please me well. For my own part, I shall be glad to learn from noble men."

Cassius shook his head. "You wrong me every way; you *wrong* me, Brutus: I said an *elder* soldier, not a 'better.'" Then uncertainty clouded his face. "Did I say 'better'?"

Brutus shrugged. "If you did, I do not care."

Cassius rallied, his eyes flashing once more. "When Caesar lived, he dared not anger me this way."

Brutus scoffed, "Peace, peace, you dared not tempt him this way."

Cassius tensed further. "I 'dared' not?"

"No."

Cassius leaped back to his feet, his hand again upon his sword. "What? *Dared* not tempt him?"

Brutus shook his head. "For your life you dared not."

Cassius strode forward until they again stood within striking distance. "Do not presume too much upon my love." He drew the sword an inch from its hilt, shaking it as he did so to make certain Brutus noticed. "I may do that I shall be sorry for."

"You *have* done that you should be sorry for." Brutus glanced down at the hint of steel and dismissed it. "There is no terror, Cassius, in your threats; for I am armed so strong in honor that they pass by me like the idle wind – which I do not respect."

Cassius shook with rage ... until he again deflated, lowered his eyes, and returned his blade to its proper place.

Brutus continued, "I did send to you for certain sums of gold – which you denied me – for *I* can raise no money by vile means. By heaven, I had rather exchange my heart and sell my blood for Greek drachmas than to wring vile trash from the hard hands of peasants by any dishonesty. I did send to you for gold to pay my legions – which you denied me. Was *that* done like Cassius? Should *I* have answered Caius Cassius like this?" He straightened his shoulders, standing tall. "When Marcus Brutus grows so covetous to lock such worthless coins from his friends, be ready, gods, with all your thunderbolts – dash him to pieces!"

"I did not deny you," Cassius insisted.

"You did."

"I did not! He was nothing but a fool that brought my answer back." He met Brutus' eyes again, but only for a handful of heartbeats before lowering his gaze once more. And when he spoke again, his voice had lost most of its fire. "Brutus has split my heart. A friend should bear his friend's infirmities, but Brutus makes mine greater than they are."

"I do not, till you practice them on me."

Cassius shook his head. "You love me not."

"I do not like your faults."

"A friendly eye could never see such 'faults.'"

"A *flatterer's* would not," Brutus countered, "though they do appear as huge as high Olympus."

Cassius opened his mouth to retort, then closed it. He shuffled away from Brutus, halting to lean against one of the tent posts. When he next spoke, his voice was a great deal softer than when he began his rant.

"Come, Antony, and young Octavius, come, revenge yourselves on Cassius alone, for Cassius is aweary of the world; hated by one he loves, defied by his brother, scolded like a bondman, all his faults observed – set in a notebook, learned, and memorized by rote in order to cast them into my teeth. Oh, I could weep my spirit from my eyes!"

Brutus said nothing, content to wait him out.

After a pregnant pause, Cassius turned and drew, not his sword, but his dagger from his belt. He held it out, handle forth, offering it to Brutus.

"There is my dagger," he said as he placed his other hand over his heart, "and here my naked breast; within, a heart worth more than Pluto's [4] mine, richer than gold." He stepped forward and shook the dagger. "If you are a Roman, take it forth. I – that denied you gold – will give my heart; strike, as you did at Caesar; for I know, when you

---

4

In Elizabethan times, Pluto – the god of the underworld – was commonly confused with Plutus – the god of wealth. Whether this instance is intentionally written as a mistake on Cassius' part, or is, in fact, an error on the part of Shakespeare himself has been the subject of some debate.

did hate him worst, you loved him better than you ever loved Cassius."

Brutus stared at Cassius – standing before him, offering his dagger in proclaimed self-sacrifice – then shook his head as the faintest hint of a smile threatened to grace his lips. "Sheathe your dagger," he sighed. "Be angry whenever you will; it shall have freedom. Do what you will, any dishonorable words shall be humored." He shook his head again and chuckled at himself. "Oh, Cassius, you are yoked with a lamb that carries anger as the flint bears fire – who, much enforced, shows a hasty spark, and straightaway is cold again."

Cassius eyed him for a moment, then put his dagger away. His gaze lowered once more, he asked, "Has Cassius lived to be nothing but mirth and laughter to his Brutus when grief and ill-tempered blood vexes him?"

Brutus shrugged. "When I spoke that, I was ill-tempered, too."

This brought some hint of comfort to Cassius' eyes as he lifted his face. "Do you confess so much?" When Brutus nodded, Cassius extended his right arm. "Give me your hand."

Brutus accepted Cassius' hand with both of his own. "And my heart, too."

Cassius' relief flourished. "Oh, Brutus!"

Brutus cocked his head. "What's the matter?"

"Do you have enough love to bear with me, when that rash temper which my mother gave me makes me forgetful?"

Brutus chuckled again as he released Cassius' hand. "Yes, Cassius; and from now on, when you are 'over-earnest' with your Brutus, he'll think your mother chides, and leave it at that."

Cassius smiled and nodded his appreciation. But before they could speak further, a harried voice from outside Brutus' tent carried through to them.

"Let me go in to see the Generals," demanded the agitated man. "There is some grudge between them; it is not appropriate they should be alone."

Brutus exchanged a concerned glance with Cassius, who had calmed enough to flush in shame; their efforts to hide their animosity from the troops had, evidently, not been as successful as they had hoped.

"You shall not come to them," they heard Lucilius state.

The would-be intruder raised his voice further. "Nothing but death shall stay me."

Taking the initiative, Cassius moved to the tent flap and opened it; Brutus followed behind him. Affecting a casual tone, Cassius inquired, "Come now, what's the matter?"

The speaker, an elderly, bedraggled man who stood before the guards, blinked in surprise, then bowed and said, "For shame, you Generals, what do you mean by this behavior?" Then he straightened, cleared this throat, and delivered in a poet's articulation, "Love, and be friends, as two such men should be; for I have seen more years, I'm sure, than ye."

Cassius froze for a second, then laughed aloud. "How vilely this rude philosopher does rhyme!"

His laughter, a welcome release after their tense argument, infected Brutus, who waved off the poor poet. "Get away, sirrah! Saucy fellow, away!"

Cassius, who recognized the unkempt, now-flustered poet, placed a calming hand upon Brutus' shoulder. "Bear with him, Brutus. It is his fashion."

Brutus shook his head, though he continued to snicker along with Cassius. "I'll humor him when he knows the proper time. What should the wars do with these dancing fools?" He waved the poet away with more force. "Base fellow, away!"

Cassius joined him in brushing the poet off. "Away, away, be gone!"

At last, flustered, the poet shuffled from the tent.

The mirth of the moment was passing, but Brutus kept his voice light as he commanded, "Lucilius and Titinius, bid the commanders prepare to encamp their companies tonight."

Cassius added to his dear friend Titinius, "And then come in yourself, and bring Messala with you, immediately to us."

Lucilius and Titinius bowed, then hurried to perform their tasks.

Brutus turned to where his servant, Lucius, had awaited on a stool outside the tent's entrance. "Lucius, a bowl of wine."

The boy nodded and rushed off just as the soldiers had.

Closing the tent flap, an awkward beat passed between the two men. Not wanting to lose the comradery they had regained, Cassius made a show of lowering himself back onto the bench in a most relaxed manner. With a chuckle, he observed, "I did not think *you* could have been so angry."

He had expected this to bring humor to Brutus' face; instead, his words had a more sobering effect on Brutus than anything he had said during their heated argument. Brutus lowered his head, drew a long, deep breath, and released it just as slowly before speaking.

"Oh, Cassius," he confessed in a weary voice, "I am sick of many griefs."

Cassius was uncertain how to respond to this sudden melancholy. After brief consideration, he chose to offer another smile and reference Brutus' long-standing practice of Stoicism. "You make no use of your philosophy, if you yield to casual misfortunes."

His renewed efforts to lift Brutus' mood again failed; if anything, Brutus grew more funereal.

"No man bears sorrow better," Brutus countered. "Portia is dead."

Cassius gasped, "Ha ...? *Portia?*"

Brutus met his eyes, his gaze bitter and mournful. In a strained, flat voice, he repeated, "She is dead."

Cassius rose onto shaky, uncertain legs; he felt as though he'd had the wind knocked from his soul. Brutus' wonderful, beautiful wife ... *dead*? In spite of all the upheaval in their lives since the ides of March, this seemed an impossible turn of events.

Cassius moved closer to his friend, reached out to grip his arm in support, but something in Brutus' bearing stayed his hand. Instead, he whispered, "How did I escape being killed when I crossed you so? Oh, insupportable and touching loss!" He shook his head. "Of what sickness?"

Brutus moved away to sit at the central table of his tent as he answered, "Unable to endure my absence, and grief that young Octavius, with Mark Antony, have made themselves so strong – for those tidings came with news of her death – with all this ... she fell to distraction and, when her attendants were absent, she ... swallowed fire."

At this, Cassius was too shocked to even gasp. "And died so?"

Brutus nodded, a slow, miserable motion. "Even so."

Cassius could not believe this. To kill oneself by swallowing burning coals? Such a terrible, anguishing manner in which to commit the act! Perhaps her attendants, whom he presumed found her body, misunderstood somehow? Perhaps Portia instead suffocated under the fumes of the hot coals by moving them, and herself, into a small, unventilated room – such as Brutus' study? Or even, much as he hated to think it, some ill-minded fool along the lines of communication had chosen to wax poetic, and dear Portia had simply swallowed poison? [5]

Then Cassius felt a wave of self-disgust to have applied "simply" to *any* method of the loss of dear Portia. Aloud, he uttered, "Oh, you immortal gods!"

Movement at the tent flaps caught the attention of both men as young Lucius entered, encumbered with the wine and some tapers. Tottering a bit, he carried his load toward the table where Brutus sat and Cassius stood.

Under his breath, Brutus said to Cassius, "Speak no more of her."

Cassius nodded his understanding, though his heart still ached at such sad news.

To the boy, Brutus commanded, "Give me a bowl of wine."

Lucius hurried to obey.

Accepting the wine, Brutus stood and raised it toward his friend. "In this I bury all unkindness, Cassius." And he took a long swallow.

Cassius offered a sincere smile at these words. "My heart is thirsty for that noble pledge. Fill, Lucius, till the wine overswells the

---

[5]

For hundreds of years, historians proclaimed that Portia killed herself by putting hot embers in her mouth. Modern historians have challenged this notion as a strange and unthinkably agonizing way in which to commit suicide. As such, suicide by carbon monoxide or by poison have been put forth, and that perhaps one of these is what Shakespeare actually intended when he wrote that Portia "swallow'd fire."

cup; I cannot drink too much of Brutus' love." And he, too, accepted and drank.

With that, Lucius hurried to light the tapers and withdraw from the tent until summoned once more. And as he exited, Titinius and Messala arrived at the entrance.

Lifting his voice, Brutus greeted them. "Come in, Titinius. Welcome, good Messala. Now we sit close about this taper here, and begin discussions of our necessities."

The two soldiers joined them, and all four moved to sit about the table.

Cassius, however, still found it difficult to focus, and without being fully aware of doing so, whispered, "Portia, are you gone?"

Among the general shuffling and chair shifting, Brutus was the only one who heard him, and he wanted to keep it that way. In an equally low voice, he said to Cassius, "No more, I pray you."

Cassius nodded, rallying his emotions back into check. They all sat, and Brutus brought the meeting to order.

"Messala," Brutus said, picking up and unrolling some scrolls, "I have here received letters that young Octavius and Mark Antony come down upon us with a mighty army, diverting their course toward Philippi."

Messala nodded. "I have letters of the same substance."

"With what addition?"

"That – by proscription and bills of outlawry – Octavius, Antony, and Lepidus have put to death a hundred Senators."

Brutus mused, "There our letters do not well agree; mine speak of seventy Senators that died by their proscriptions, Cicero being one."

Cassius blurted in surprise, "*Cicero* one?" While Cassius himself had proposed including Cicero in their assassination plans, Brutus had overruled him; therefore, elderly Cicero had been innocent of any wrongdoing. *None* of the other Senators had anything to do with the conspirators' plans!

Messala confirmed, "Cicero is dead, and by that order of proscription." To Brutus, he asked, with some hesitation, "Have you any letters from your wife, my lord?"

Cassius shot a wary glance toward Brutus, but his friend betrayed no reaction other than to answer, "No, Messala."

Messala persisted, "Nor nothing in your other letters written of her?"

"Nothing, Messala."

Messala appeared at a loss. In a low voice, he said, "That, I think, is strange."

As Cassius watched in awe, Brutus – his face a mask of neutrality – responded, "Why do you ask? Have you heard anything of her in yours?"

Flustered, Messala averted his gaze. "No, my lord."

But Brutus would not let that go. "Now, as you are a Roman, tell me true."

Messala steeled himself, then said, "Then, like a Roman, bear the truth I tell: For certain ... Portia is dead, and by strange manner."

A moment of silence followed this "revelation," with Messala and Titinius waiting with uncomfortable, held breath, while Cassius continued to observe in confused amazement over Brutus' strange performance.

At last, Brutus placed his hands upon the tabletop; he closed his eyes and declared in a steady voice, "Why, farewell, Portia." He then opened his eyes, looked at Messala across from him, and all but shrugged as he said, "We all must die, Messala. After meditating that she must die eventually, I have the fortitude to endure it now."

Messala spoke in deep admiration, "In such a way, great men should endure great losses."

Cassius realized that, whereas Brutus had allowed his emotions to gain the better of him during their private conversation, *this* was Brutus practicing the Stoicism he had embraced for so long. He admitted aloud, "I have put as much into this philosophical art as you, and yet my nature could not bear it so."

Messala and Titinius nodded their earnest agreement, and Brutus inclined his head, accepting their praise with an appreciative smile. [6]

After a pregnant pause, Brutus gave the table a light slap. "Well, to our work which concerns the living. What do you think of marching to Philippi immediately?"

Cassius spoke up. "I do not think it good."

"Your reason?"

"This is it: It is better that the enemy seek us; so shall he waste his means, weary his soldiers, do offense to himself; while we, lying still, are full of rest, defense, and nimbleness."

But Brutus countered, "Good reasons must of necessity give place to better: The people between Philippi and this ground do stand with us in a forced affection, for they have begrudged us contribution. The enemy, marching along by them, shall make up a fuller number *from* them, come on refreshed, reinforced, and encouraged – we shall cut them off from this advantage if we do face them there at Philippi, these people at our back."

Cassius shook his head. "Hear me, good brother—"

6

Brutus' odd behavior of pretending to Messala that he knew nothing of Portia's death, in spite of having already described it to Cassius, has been much debated. Taken as it is written, Brutus appears to be putting on a "show of strength" for the troops, whereas he had allowed himself to be more vulnerable in Cassius' company; or, from a more cynical viewpoint, that Brutus set the latter stage specifically to bask in the flattering admiration of Messala and Titinius – thus showcasing Brutus' vanity.

Another alternative has been proposed: That Shakespeare wrote the latter passage first, showing Brutus receiving the news in proper "Stoic" fashion, but at some point the playwright realized that this detached conduct – perfectly acceptable to ancient Romans – would seem too cold and uncaring to his English audiences (many films and modern stage adaptations omit the latter "Stoic" reaction altogether). Therefore, Shakespeare then wrote the former passage, wherein Brutus displayed a far more emotional reaction to his wife's death. If this theory holds, this suggests that both versions were preserved in the Folio text in error, and were never intended to appear in the play together.

Brutus cut him off with a slight raise of his voice. "I beg your pardon."

Cassius – having no desire to test Brutus again so soon – backed down, gesturing for him to continue.

"You must note besides that we have drawn the utmost from our friends, our legions are brim full, our cause is ripe. The enemy increases every day; we, at our height, are ready to decline." Brutus passed his gaze across all three men. "There is a tide in the affairs of men which, taken at the flood, leads on to fortune; if neglected, all the voyage of their life is confined to shallows and in miseries. We are now afloat on such a full sea, and we must take the current when it serves, or lose everything."

After a brief consideration, and with no other suggestions to propose, Cassius stated, "Then, as you wish, go on; we'll go along ourselves, and meet them at Philippi."

Messala and Titinius exchanged looks, then nodded their own agreement.

Brutus accepted their concurrence, then glanced around the darkened tent. "The deep of night has crept upon our talk, and nature must obey necessity – which we will dole out with a little rest." He looked to Cassius. "There is no more to say?"

Cassius shook his head. "No more. Goodnight." He stood, and the others followed suit. "Early tomorrow we will rise, and go hence."

Brutus nodded, then called, "Lucius!"

The boy appeared in seconds.

"My sleeping gown," Brutus ordered.

Lucius bowed and stepped through a privacy partition in the tent structure.

Then Brutus addressed his fellows. "Farewell, good Messala ... Goodnight, Titinius ..." To Cassius, he reached out to place a friendly hand upon his shoulder. "Noble, noble Cassius, goodnight and good repose."

Cassius returned the gesture. "Oh, my dear brother! This was an ill beginning of the night. May such division never come between our souls! Let it not, Brutus."

Lucius had produced Brutus' sleeping gown and waited in silence for his master to conclude his farewells for the night.

Brutus reassured Cassius, "Everything is well."

Cassius bowed his head in thanks. "Goodnight, my lord."

"Goodnight, good brother."

Titinius and Messala both said, "Goodnight, Lord Brutus."

Releasing Cassius, he waved to them all. "Farewell, everyone."

And with that, Brutus and patient Lucius were alone.

Brutus reached out. "Give me the gown." As he took it and began stripping for the night, he asked his servant, "Where is your musical instrument?"

"Here in the tent," Lucius answered with a gesture to the partition; as he did so, he stifled a yawn.

"What, you speak drowsily?" Brutus teased. When Lucius attempted to deny it, he added, "Poor knave, I do not blame you; you are exhausted." He then instructed the boy, "Call Claudio and some other of my men; I'll have them sleep on cushions in my tent."

Lucius bowed and moved to open the tent's entrance flap. "Varrus and Claudio!" [7] he called, then hastened to ready the cushions.

The summoned servants appeared with almost as much alacrity as Lucius. They each bowed, and Varrus asked, "Calls my lord?"

"I pray you, sirs," Brutus answered, "lie in my tent and sleep. It may be I shall rouse you soon on business to my brother Cassius."

Again they each bowed, and again Varrus spoke. "If it so pleases you, we will stand awake and await your command."

But Brutus dismissed that. "I will not have it so." He gestured toward the cushions Lucius had produced. "Lie down, good sirs. It may be I shall change my mind."

As the men prepared their cushions, Brutus slipped on his sleeping gown; he noticed that it was overweighted to one side and,

---

[7] *While different character spellings frequently appear in the various surviving editions of Shakespeare's works, my research found even less consistency with the servants summoned in this scene: "Varrus" is sometimes "Varro," while "Claudio" is alternately "Cladio" or even "Claudius" (a name most associated with* Hamlet*), and all the assorted editions mix-and-match them. For this novelization, I chose to follow the Riverside Shakespeare with "Varrus" and "Claudio."*

dipping his hand into that pocket, discovered something that amused him.

"Look, Lucius," he showed the boy, "here's the book I sought for so. I put it in the pocket of my gown."

Lucius attempted to hide his smirk of vindication, without complete success. In as measured a tone as his age could muster, he said, "I was sure your Lordship did not give it to me."

Brutus chuckled at that. "Bear with me, good boy, I am very forgetful. Can you hold up your heavy eyes awhile and touch your instrument a strain or two?"

Lucius nodded. "Aye, my lord, if it pleases you."

"It does, my boy. I trouble you too much, but you are always willing."

Lucius offered a bashful shrug and a smile. "It is my duty, sir."

Brutus sighed. "I should not urge your duty past your endurance. I know young bloods yearn for a time of rest."

Lucius shrugged again. "I have slept, my lord, already."

This made Brutus chuckle once more. "It was well done, and you shall sleep again. I will not hold you long." Then he grew a touch more serious, and to himself, he added, "If I do live, I will be good to you."

And so Lucius retrieved his lute as Brutus reclined upon his sleeping couch. The boy strummed his instrument and intoned a sweet melody.

This is a sleepy tune, Brutus reflected. He basked in the sound, considered the book in his hand and the day to follow, the upcoming conflict at Philippi and the questions of – win or lose this battle – what came next ...

Eventually, he realized that Lucius had stopped singing. To his only mild surprise, he discovered that the boy had fallen asleep, still holding his lute.

He observed the sleeping boy, so motionless he scarcely seemed to breathe. *Oh, murderous slumber! You lay your heavy mace upon my boy, that plays you music?*

"Gentle boy," he whispered as he set his book aside, "goodnight; I will not do you so much wrong to wake you. If you do nod, you will break your instrument. I'll take it from you and, good boy, goodnight."

With great and gentle care, Brutus eased the lute from the boy's grasp and lowered sleeping Lucius down onto his own couch. Setting the lute near his head, he collected his book and moved back to his table where the taper still burned.

"Let me see ... let me see ..." he muttered under his breath as he sat and held the book into the light, "... is the leaf not turned down where I left off reading? Here it is, I think." He leaned forward, edging the book closer to the taper.

Soon, the dim light, the lingering memory of Lucius' sweet tune, the long day with his quarrel with Cassius, and the daunting confrontation all colluded to set weights upon Brutus' own eyes, and he found himself losing focus on the words on the page, his breath slowing ... his head resting against his fist ... then threatening to slide down, to alight upon the tabletop, which had never tempted him so ...

Then movement crossed his field of vision – what little there was left, peeking from beneath his ponderous eyelids. Brutus rallied himself, pushing back to something closer to wakefulness, but it was difficult.

He glanced around the tent, finding it much darker than expected. *How poorly this taper burns ...* It was almost as if—

Then his eyes gazed upon the source of the motion he had detected, and he no longer found it quite so arduous to awaken.

"Ha ..." he gasped. "Who comes here?" He scrubbed at his face and shook his head in denial. "I think it is the weakness of my eyes that shapes this monstrous apparition. It comes toward me."

The shape displayed across from the table resembled congealed smoke as much as it did flesh ... but Brutus recognized it as the ghost of Caesar!

If it were, in fact, what it appeared to be.

"Are you anything?" he asked in a strained whisper. "Are you some god, some angel, or some devil, that makes my blood cold and my hair stand?" When the vision neither replied nor moved, he demanded, "Speak to me what you are."

And thus, the ghost of Caesar spoke, *"Your evil spirit, Brutus."*

Winded by receiving such an answer, Brutus licked his dry lips. "Why do you come?"

"*To tell you,*" it answered, "*you shall see me at Philippi.*"

This was it, then. Brutus had never – not in his heart of hearts – believed in ghosts, before now. But he trusted his senses, and he accepted the terrible wrong he had committed upon this poor, great man who wavered before him; there was little use in denying it. If such a haunting were intertwined with his fate, then so be it – he would not balk.

Grasping for every shred of Stoicism he had ever practiced, he said, "Well; then I shall see you again?"

The ghost nodded. "*Aye, at Philippi.*"

Brutus stood, a cautious, unsteady motion. "Why," he said, closing his eyes as he grappled with his useless fear, "I will see you at Philippi, then."

Mastering himself, he opened his eyes to ask more of his dear, murdered friend, his victim ...

But the ghost was gone.

Somehow, this sudden absence stung Brutus' core more than its appearance. "Now that I have taken heart," he sputtered, "you vanish." Moving around the table, he raised his voice, demanding, "Ill spirit, I would hold more talk with you."

Nothing.

Had it all been a figment of his imagination? Was his mind growing addled under the pressure they faced? Brutus shuddered to think so; better to face a true ghost than the failing of his faculties.

Perhaps he had dreamed it? Perhaps one of those sleeping here in the tent had disturbed his sleep in some manner, prompting this vision?

Or ... perhaps there might be *witnesses* to this apparition?

"Boy, Lucius!" he called out. "Varrus! Claudio! Sirs, awake! Claudio!"

All of Brutus' tent-mates stirred at once. Lucius, for his part, jolted upright, his hands flailing in front of him, his fingers making plucking motions.

"The strings, my lord," the boy mumbled, "are out of tune ..."

He thinks he is still at his instrument, Brutus thought. He hurried over to the boy and spoke aloud, "Lucius, awake!"

Lucius shook his head, blinking his eyes up at his master. "My lord?"

"Did you dream, Lucius, that you cried out so?"

Lucius appeared quite confused. "My lord, I do not know that I did cry."

"Yes, that you did," Brutus insisted, knowing that he did so without true merit. Then he asked, "Did you *see* anything?"

Lucius shook his head. "Nothing, my lord."

Grunting in frustration, Brutus snapped, "Sleep again, Lucius." He then rushed over to his two man-servants, who had sat up but were still more than half asleep. He leaned over one, "You, Claudio!" Then he leaned over the other. "Fellow you, awake!"

The men stumbled to their feet, bowing.

"My lord?"

"My lord?"

Brutus all but shook the men. "Why did you cry out so, sirs, in your sleep?"

The men exchanged bewildered looks, and together asked, "Did we, my lord?"

"Aye," Brutus maintained, though he felt his tangible excuses slipping through his fingers. "Did you see anything?"

"No, my lord," said Varrus, "I saw nothing."

Claudio agreed, "Nor I, my lord."

Brutus realized that he was sweating, and that all of them – Lucius, Varrus, Claudio – were staring at him with heavy concern, and a strong dash of fear.

Nothing having disturbed his sleep; no witnesses to any supernatural phenomenon. Only his force of will prevented Brutus from shuddering once again.

With a raspy voice, he commanded the men, "Go, and convey greetings to my brother Cassius; bid him set forth his troops soon before us, and we will follow."

Grateful for an exchange they could understand, the men bowed and said together, "It shall be done, my lord." They hurried from the tent.

Brutus turned to find Lucius awaiting, expectant of his own

orders; no judgment lurked behind the boys eyes, simply the loyalty that resided there, always.

Without a word, Brutus removed his sleeping gown and, passing it to Lucius, moved to don his armor.

PART FIVE

CHAPTER ONE

Marcus Antony reclined upon one of the few hillets, doing his best to relax here on these expansive, bland plains near Philippi. His forces had paused to assess their situation before meeting their enemies in combat; he and Octavius possessed the greater army, to be sure, but the traitors Brutus and Cassius held superior positioning up in the hills.

Antony and his allies could not remain in this lowly flat-land indefinitely, inviting eventual hunger and fatigue; yet, the notion of retreat irked Antony. Thus, he awaited inspiration.

Running footsteps drew his attention, and he found his fellow Triumvir Octavius rushing toward him, the lad's face alight with dark pleasure. Releasing a begrudging sigh over this interruption of his gentle repose, Antony stood to greet him.

Before they had even come together, Octavius shouted, "Now, Antony, our hopes are answered!"

He reached the hillet, winded but too excited to wait for his breath to return.

"You said the enemy would not come down, but keep the hills and upper regions." His smile widened as he huffed. "It proves not so: Their battalions are at hand; they mean to challenge us here at Philippi, answering before we do challenge them."

Antony mused over this, then released a dismissive grunt. "Tut, I am in their hearts, and I know why they do it: They would prefer to be anywhere else, and come down with false bravery, thinking by this pretense to fasten in our thoughts that they have 'courage.' " He chuckled, a malicious sound. "But it is not so."

In Octavius' wake, a messenger dashed toward them, his

demeanor more frantic than Octavius' before him. "Prepare yourselves, Generals! The enemy comes on in gallant show. Their bloody sign for combat is hung out, and something to be done immediately."

Antony nodded his understanding and waved the messenger away. He was surprised by this tactical error – some might call it egregious stupidity! – on the part of Brutus and Cassius, but he was more than pleased to take advantage of it.

Hands on his hips, he considered the proximal grounds, then nodded. "Octavius, lead your battalions slowly on upon the left hand of the even field." Order issued, he bent to collect his sheathed gladius sword.

But rather than hurrying off as expected, Octavius remained. When Antony faced the younger man, he found Octavius' face inscrutable. "I will go upon the *right* hand," he told Antony. "You keep the left."

Antony studied Octavius, but his eyes were as cryptic as his expression. "Why do you cross me during this urgency?"

Octavius shrugged. "I do not 'cross' you, but I will do as I have stated." And off he marched.

Antony considered calling him back, but the sound of drums convinced him that this was not the time; he would deal with Octavius' growing impertinence another day. With a shading hand over his brow, he saw with his own eyes that the enemy's forces – the fools – were indeed coming down from their higher ground.

*   *   *

Leading the way at an easy pace, Brutus and Cassius guided their horses side by side, with Lucilius, Titinius, and Messala close behind. Brutus took in the formations below, and observed Antony and Octavius calling their forces to a premature halt. They stood upon the would-be battleground, waiting.

Brutus drew back his steed; Cassius followed suit, and their entire army matched them.

Brutus commented, "They stand, and would have parley."

Cassius nodded, then called back over his shoulder, "Stand fast,

Titinius. We must go out and talk."

Titinius nodded and held up his arms in the appropriate signal. With a wary, and weary, glance to one another, Brutus and Cassius proceeded down to the plain.

As Antony and Octavius awaited their arrival, Octavius leaned toward his ally. "Mark Antony, shall we give sign of battle?"

"No, Octavius Caesar, we will retaliate upon their charge." Antony inclined his head toward their enemies. "Go forth. The 'Generals' would have some words."

Octavius turned to his officers. "Do not stir until the signal."

And so Antony and Octavius rode forward to meet Brutus and Cassius.

When the four came together, it was Brutus who spoke first. "Words before blows; is it so, countrymen?"

Octavius countered, "Not that we love words better, as you do."

Brutus eyed him with open distaste. "Good words are better than *bad strokes*, Octavius."

Antony barked bitter laughter at that. "In your 'bad strokes,' Brutus, you give good words; witness the hole you made in Caesar's heart, crying 'Long live, hail, Caesar'!"

Cassius fumed, "Antony, the posture of your blows are yet unknown. But for *your* words ... they rob the Sicilian Hybla bees and leave them honeyless."

Antony smirked. "Not stingless, too?"

"Oh, yes," Brutus cut in, "and *soundless*, too; for you have stolen their buzzing, Antony, and very wisely threaten before you sting."

Antony sneered, "Villains! You did not do so when your vile daggers hacked one another in the sides of Caesar. Grinning, you showed your teeth like apes, and fawned like hounds, and bowed like bondmen – kissing Caesar's feet! While damned Casca, like a cur, struck Caesar from behind on the neck." He growled, "Oh, you hypocrites!"

" 'Hypocrites'?" Cassius spat, thinking of Cicero and the dozens of other Senators who had died at this man's hand. He snapped at his friend, "Now, Brutus, thank *yourself*." He pointed at Antony. "This tongue would not have offended so today if *Cassius* might have prevailed."

Brutus said nothing to that. He was well aware – painfully, so – that it was his word which had prevented the conspirators from killing Antony, too, on the ides of March. His own nobility, as much as anything, led to these particular circumstances.

"Come, come," interjected Octavius, "to the cause at hand! If arguing makes us sweat, the test of it will turn to redder drops." He seized his gladius, jerked it forth, and held it high so that his army could witness, calling back, "Look, I draw a sword against conspirators!" He whirled back to Brutus and Cassius. "When do you think the sword goes back into its sheath? *Never*, till Caesar's three-and-thirty wounds [8] are well avenged, or till *another* Caesar has been slaughtered by the sword of traitors!"

Brutus shook his head. "Octavius Caesar, you cannot die by traitors' hands ..." He peered up at Octavius' aloft sword. "... unless you bring them against yourself."

"So I hope;" Octavius returned, "I was not born to die on *Brutus'* sword."

"Oh, if you were the noblest of your family line, young man," Brutus countered, "you could not die more honorably."

"A peevish schoolboy," Cassius scoffed, "worthless of such honor ..." He turned his gaze to Antony. "... joined with a masquerader and a reveler!"

Antony laughed at this attempt to insult his pastimes. "Old Cassius still!"

But Octavius had reached his limit. "Come, Antony, away!" he snarled. To Brutus and Cassius, he growled, "Traitors, we hurl our defiance in your teeth. If you dare fight today, come to the field; if not, when you have stomachs for it."

With that, Octavius pulled his horse around and rode back to his lines; Antony smirked at Brutus and Cassius, then followed after him.

Cassius sounded tired and depressed as he watched their

---

[8]

A few editions have corrected this number to "three-and-twenty," as this is considered by some to be more historically accurate. I have defaulted to the traditional majority of "three-and-thirty."

enemies leave. "Why now, blow, you wind; swell, you waves; and swim, you ships! The storm is up, and all is at stake."

Brutus offered no reply to this as they, too, turned back to rejoin their ranks. But as they drew near, he called, "Ho, Lucilius, hark, a word with you."

Lucilius brought his horse forward to meet them, followed by Messala.

"My lord?" Lucilius said.

Brutus gestured to Lucilius, and the two of them trotted their horses off to one side for a private word, leaving Cassius and Messala together a short distance before the front line.

After a long moment of silence, Cassius said, "Messala."

Messala perked up. "What says my General?"

At first, it seemed as though Cassius might say nothing at all. Finally, in a low voice, he spoke, "Messala, this is my birthday, as this very day Cassius was born. Give me your hand, Messala." Messala, caught somewhat off-guard by the request, indulged him. "You be my witness that against my will – as Pompey was, at the battle of Pharsalia – I am compelled to set all our liberties upon this one battle." He drew a fatigued breath. "You know that I held Epicurus, and his opinion, strong ..."

Messala nodded. Epicurus of Samos, the Greek philosopher, considered "omens" and "divine portents" to be nothing more than empty superstition.

Cassius smiled, though it was joyless. "Now I change my mind, and partly credit things that do presage. Coming from Sardis, two mighty eagles swooped down on our foremost banner, and there they perched – gorging and feeding from our soldiers' hands, who accompanied us here to Philippi." He sighed. "This morning the eagles are fled away and gone, and in their place ravens, crows, and kites do fly over our heads and look downward on us as if we were sickly prey. Their shadows seem a most foreboding canopy, under which our army lies, ready to give up the ghost."

Messala, uncomfortable with such a discussion before a great battle, could only respond with a feeble entreaty, "Do not believe so."

Cassius studied the man's disconcerted expression; he then forced a chuckle, which sounded much lighter than he felt. "I only believe it partly," he reassured the soldier, "for I am fresh of spirit, and resolved to meet all perils very constantly."

Messala did not seem truly assuaged by the sudden improvement in Cassius' mood, but any further reply was cut short as Brutus and Lucilius returned.

"... even so, Lucilius," Brutus was concluding as he brought his steed to a halt and slid down from its back.

Cassius joined him in bringing his feet to earth. "Now, most noble Brutus," he proclaimed, "may the gods stand friendly today, that we – lovers of peace – may lead on our days to old age. But since the affairs of men rest still uncertain, let's consider the worst that may befall." He held his head high. "If we do lose this battle, then this is the very last time we shall speak together: What are you then determined to do?"

Brutus gave his reply due deliberation before answering, "Even by the rule of that philosophy by which I did blame Cato of Utica, my father-in-law, for the death which he did give himself – I do not know how, but I do find it cowardly and vile, for fear of what *might* fall, to cut short the time of life – arming myself with patience ..." He, too, held his head high. "... to await the providence of some higher powers that govern us below."

"Then, if we lose this battle," Cassius clarified, "you are contented to be led, as a captive bound in fetters, through the streets of Rome?"

Brutus mulled this over, then shook his head. "No, Cassius, no. Do not think, you noble Roman, that Brutus will *ever* go bound to Rome; he bears too great a mind. But this same day must end that work the ides of March begun. And whether we shall meet again, I do not know. Therefore ..." He reached out his open hand. "... take our everlasting farewell."

Cassius clasped his offered hand in a firm grip, and they each took the other by the forearm as well.

"Forever and forever farewell, Cassius," Brutus declared. "If we do meet again, why, we shall smile." And he did so. "If not ... why then, this parting was well made."

Cassius could not quite match his smile, but his emotions stood clear in his eyes. "Forever and forever farewell, Brutus. If we do meet again, we'll smile indeed; if not, it is true this parting was well made."

Brutus gave his hand one more, firm shake, then released him and clapped him upon the shoulder. "Why then, lead on."

Nodding together, they regarded the forces opposing them.

"Oh," Brutus said, "that a man might know the end of this day's business before it comes! But it suffices that the day *will* end, and then the end is known." He clapped Cassius' shoulder once more. "Come ho, away!"

PART FIVE

CHAPTER TWO

The battle was engaged. And, to Brutus' eyes, appeared to be going quite well.

Cassius' forces had taken the seaside against Antony, while Brutus led his army on the inland side opposing Octavius. And Octavius was beginning to falter.

Brutus saw his opportunity.

Riding through the fighting and calls-to-arms that sounded across the plains, Brutus brought his steed alongside Messala's.

Withdrawing hastily-crafted scrolls from within his armor, Brutus pointed toward Cassius' seaside wing. "Ride," he commanded, "ride, Messala, ride, and give these written orders unto the legions on the other side!"

He shoved the scrolls into Messala's hand even as another loud call-to-arms resonated.

"Let Cassius set on at once," he urged, "for I perceive nothing but cold faint-heartedness in Octavius' wing, and a sudden push shall overthrow them." He clapped his hands, though the din of battle consumed most of it. "Ride, ride, Messala, let them all come down!"

Messala rode away, and Brutus surveyed the death occurring before him ... but most of that death fell to Octavius' men.

Victory awaited this day!

CHAPTER THREE

Disaster struck this day.

Calls-to-arms continued, but not for Cassius; Cassius no longer had an army left to answer that call.

Leading his horse on foot, trudging back up to the hills – the hills which they never should have left! – Cassius himself carried the standard for his forces. He heard other footsteps plodding behind him and presumed they belonged to loyal Titinius, but by now nothing would surprise him.

Upon reaching a plateau, Cassius released his horse's reins and slumped against a rock to regain his strength. And, looking back out over the field of war, his face soured in disgust.

"Oh, look, Titinius," he said, pointing toward their scattered, fleeing troops, "look, the villains fly! I myself have turned into the enemy of my own troops." He shook the standard once, before laying it against the rock. "That standard-bearer of mine was turning back; I slew the coward, and did take the flag from him."

"Oh, Cassius," Titinius groaned, "Brutus gave the word too early, who – having some advantage on Octavius – took it too eagerly. His soldiers fell to looting, while we are all enclosed by Antony."

More stumbling footsteps approached from downhill. Both Cassius and Titinius had drawn their swords before recognizing that it was their own Pindarus who stumbled toward them.

The bloody, exhausted young man collapsed to one knee before them, gasping as he warned, "Fly further off, my lord, fly further off ... Mark Antony is in your tents, my lord ... therefore fly, noble Cassius, fly far off ..."

Cassius reached down to touch the man's shoulder in gratitude, and told him, "This hill is far enough."

Pindarus nodded his understanding, then resumed catching his breath.

Sheathing his sword, Cassius stepped forward and peered down at the debacle below. His eyesight not being as reliable in recent years, he waved Titinius over. "Look, look, Titinius ... are those my tents where I perceive the fire?"

Titinius sighed, "They are, my lord."

Cassius shook his head; everything was falling apart.

"Titinius," he said, pointing toward another portion of the battlefields, "if you love me, you mount my horse and hide your spurs in him till he has brought you up to yonder troops and here again, so that I may rest assured whether yonder troops are friend, or enemy."

Good Titinius, loyal Titinius, responded, "I will be here again as quick as a thought." The noble soldier hurried to Cassius' tired horse, mounted, and rode off.

Cassius glanced at the slope above him, judged his energy reserves, and found them wanting; that, plus his eyesight grew weaker along with his drained body. Instead, he ordered the younger man, "Go, Pindarus, get higher on that hill. My sight was ever dull. Observe Titinius and tell me what you note about the field."

Pindarus climbed back to his feet and, with a bow of his head, struggled further up the hill for a better view.

Left alone with his thoughts, Cassius returned to leaning against the rock, pondering these events on this, his very birthday. *This day I first breathed: Time has come round, and where I did begin, there I shall end; my life has completed its circle.*

Unless ...

Calling up to Pindarus, he asked, "Boy, what news?"

Pindarus' voice drifted down, "Oh, my lord!"

"What *news?*"

"Titinius is enclosed round about with horsemen, that rush toward him ... yet he spurs on ... now they are almost on him ... Now, Titinius!"

Cassius hurried forth to peer down as best he could.

Pindarus continued, "Now some dismount ... oh, he dismounts, too ..." A longer pause, then, "He's *taken* ... and hark, they shout for joy."

Cassius also heard it. That was it, then.

"Come down," he called, "behold no more." Once again, he slumped against the rock, his eyes wet. *Oh, coward that I am, to live so long to see my best friend taken before my face!*

Pindarus joined him on the plateau; Cassius stared at the young man a heavy moment before speaking ... then released a long, resolute sigh, his decision made.

"Come hither, boy."

Pindarus, hearing the severe tone, drew closer and knelt before him.

"In Parthia, eleven years ago," Cassius said, "I did take you prisoner, and then I made you swear, when I spared your life, that whatsoever I did bid you do, you should attempt it." He stood from the rock once more, looking down upon Pindarus. "Come now, keep your oath."

As Pindarus rose in horror, Cassius drew his gladius and presented it to him, hilt-forth.

"Now be a free man," Cassius commanded, "and with this good sword, that ran through Caesar's bowels ..." He placed his hand upon his own chest. "... probe this bosom."

Pindarus shook his head and made as if to speak.

"Do not stand against me," Cassius snapped. "Here, you take the hilt ..."

Pindarus accepted the sword and Cassius reached back, pulling what was left of his armor's cape forward.

"... and when my face is covered, as it is now ..."

He pulled the dirty fabric over his eyes, so that he could not see Pindarus, or the deadly blade.

At last prepared, he concluded, "... you guide the sword."

And so Cassius awaited.

Pindarus did not want to do this terrible thing; yet, honor offered him no alterative. Gripping the hilt so that his knuckles whitened, he plunged the sword into his master's chest.

A startled wheeze issued from Cassius. The Roman collapsed to his knees, his face again exposed and his hand touching the sword in an almost affectionate manner.

"Caesar ..." Cassius whispered into the sky above, "... you are revenged ... even with the sword that killed you ..."

And then Cassius spoke no more.

Pindarus stared down at Cassius' body, his limbs numb with the shock of this act, and of this day. *So I am free, yet would not have been so, had I dared done my will. Oh, Cassius, Pindarus shall run far from this country, where never any Roman shall see him.*

Pindarus fled ...

Very little time passed before more footsteps sounded up the hillside as Titinius appeared – a victory wreath upon his head – guiding Messala.

"... it is nothing but an exchange, Titinius," Messala was explaining in fair spirits, "for Octavius is overthrown by noble Brutus' power, as Cassius' legions are by Antony."

Titinius declared with relief, "These tidings will comfort Cassius well."

"Where did you leave him?"

"All disconsolate, with Pindarus his bondman, on this hill."

Then Messala came to an abrupt halt. "Is that not he that lies upon the ground?"

Titinius' eyes widened. "He does not lie like the living." He collapsed to his knees. "Oh, my heart!"

Messala fumbled for the words to speak, but all he could do was repeat, "Is that not he?"

Titinius shook his head. "No ... this *was* he, Messala, but Cassius is no more." He suppressed a sob, then spoke further, "Oh, setting sun, as in your red rays you do sink to night ... so, in his red blood, Cassius' day is set. The sun of *Rome* is set! Our day is gone; clouds, infectious dews, and dangers come; our deeds are done." He shook his head, then covered his face in sorrow. "Mistrust of my success has done this deed."

Messala rested a comforting hand upon the man's neck. "Mistrust of *good* success has done this deed," he corrected. "Oh, hateful error, melancholy's child, why do you show to the gullible thoughts of men the things that are not? Oh, error, soon conceived, you never come unto a *happy* birth, but kill the mother-melancholy that bred you!"

Then Titinius lowered his hands and looked around. "What, Pindarus? Where are you, Pindarus?"

"Seek him, Titinius, while I go to meet the noble Brutus, thrusting this report into his ears. I may say 'thrusting it,' for piercing steel and envenomed darts shall be as welcome to the ears of Brutus as tidings of this sight."

Titinius nodded. "You hurry, Messala, and I will seek Pindarus for the while."

Messala returned his nod, stole one more look at Cassius, then descended the hill.

Alone, Titinius approached his dear, dead friend. "Why did you send me forth, brave Cassius? Did I not meet your friends, and did they not put on my brow this wreath of victory and bid me give it you? Did you not hear their shouts?" He leaned against the rock which had last supported Cassius in life. "Alas, you have misconstrued everything. But wait, take this garland on your brow. Your Brutus bid me give it to you, and I will do his bidding."

Removing the wreath, he leaned forward and placed it upon Cassius' still head. Then his eyes fell upon the sword, still resting in Cassius' chest.

"Brutus, come soon, and see how I regarded Caius Cassius."

Reaching out, he pulled the sword from Cassius' body.

"By your leave, gods! This is a Roman's duty."

Shifting his grip, he rotated the sword so that the blade pointed at his own chest.

"Come, Cassius' sword, and find Titinius' heart!"

His arms jerked inward ... and Titinius joined his friend, still upon the earth.

More fighting, more calls-to-arms, more bloodshed ...

Finally, Brutus and Messala mounted the hill, accompanied by

Lucilius, young Cato, Strato, Volumnius, Labio, and Flavius [9]. And a somber climb it was.

In spite of his treasured philosophy, Brutus could not quite contain his emotions as he asked, "Where, *where*, Messala, does his body lie?"

Messala pointed ahead, toward the rock. "Look, yonder, and Titinius mourning it."

Brutus slowed his stride, his head cocking to one side as he noted, "Titinius' face is upward."

Cato hurried ahead, skidding to a halt over the two dead men. Looking back to Brutus, he stammered, "He is ... slain."

Brutus and the others reached young Cato's side, and all stared down at such terrible death. None spoke at first, until Brutus at last released a weary groan.

"Oh, Julius Caesar," he said, "you are mighty yet! Your spirit walks abroad, and turns our swords into our own individual entrails."

Below, another call-to-arms sounded, but it failed to rouse these men from their grief.

Cato shook his head. "Brave Titinius!" He pointed. "See how he has crowned dead Cassius."

Brutus saw, and approved. "Are there yet two Romans living such as these?" He shook his head. "The last of all the Romans, fare you well. It is impossible that ever Rome should breed your equal."

---

[9]

Labio (sometimes "Labeo") enters the scene with the others, never speaks, is only addressed by Brutus near the very end of the scene, and his name does not appear on the play's Dramatis Personae. The same goes for Flavius – whom I initially perceived as being the Tribune from the opening of the play, but who is sometimes named "Flavio" here (another name absent from the Dramatis Personae).

Some productions choose to omit these characters entirely, framing the later dialogue so that Brutus is not issuing orders directly to Labio/Labeo and Flavius/Flavio, but is instead describing his upcoming plans to his officers.

I have chosen to keep the characters intact here, but have also honored their omission from the Dramatis Personae.

Then he rallied himself, drawing as tall as he could manage.

"Friends," he said, "I owe more tears to this dead man than you shall see me pay." He glanced back down to his friend and promised, "I shall find time, Cassius; I shall find time." Then he raised his head once more. "Come, therefore, and send his body to the island of Thasos. His funeral shall not be in our camp, for fear it discomfort us."

They all nodded their understanding.

Brutus clapped his hands twice. "Lucilius, come; and come, young Cato; let us return to the field. Labio and Flavius, set our battles onward."

He looked to the fighting below.

"It is three o'clock, and, Romans, before night ... we shall try our fortune in a second fight."

PART FIVE

CHAPTER FOUR

The renewed battle was not going well.

Brutus defeated Octavius; Antony defeated Cassius. But now that Brutus and Antony were locked in combat ...

Brutus had been sure he would triumph. Thanks to the first round of their conflict – Cassius' struggles had not been in vain – Brutus' forces controlled any approach by sea. Thus, Antony and Octavius were cut off from supplies, *if* Brutus' forces could hold their position.

Their position, however, was not holding.

Time and again, Antony drove Brutus back, and back, until finally Brutus was forced to retreat toward the hills.

Back toward where Cassius had died.

But still Brutus fought on, fought to make Antony pay for every inch of their retreat, if only he could keep his men rallied.

Surrounded by more calls-to-arms, Brutus – accompanied by faithful Messala, Cato, Lucilius, and Flavius – encouraged all of his soldiers within earshot to fight, to *fight*!

Reaching an area where his men appeared especially dejected, Brutus leaped onto a fallen tree and called out, "Now, countrymen! Oh, yet hold up your heads!"

Their response was lackluster at best. Did they not grasp the importance of this crucial battle?

Frustrated, Brutus moved on, seeking more enthusiastic brothers-in-arms, and Messala and Flavius trailed after. Lucilius made to follow suit, until he realized that young Cato had taken Brutus' place upon the tree.

"Who is so base as not to do so?" he shamed the exhausted,

crestfallen soldiers. He drew his sword and held it aloft. "Who will go with me? I will proclaim my name about the field. I am the son of Marcus Cato, ho! A foe to tyrants, and my country's friend." He stabbed at the heavens with his blade. "*I* am the *son* of *Marcus Cato*, ho!"

This was followed by an instant stir ... but not the sort for which Cato and Lucilius might have hoped.

Before Brutus' men could rally in proper fashion, Antony's forces – alongside what remained of Octavius' soldiers – broke through the crumbling lines and fell upon them. The fighting was bitter, but it was clear that Brutus' troops would falter.

Desperate, Lucilius looked to where his leader had departed. Was Brutus yet far enough away? Or might Antony capture him here, now?

No. No, he could not allow that.

Cato had launched from the tree to join the fighting, and so it was that Lucilius was the third Roman to mount it.

"And *I* am *Brutus*," Lucilius cried, "*Marcus Brutus*, I! *Brutus*, my country's friend! Know me for *Brutus*!" [10]

The struggle intensified, as Lucilus had hoped – for so long as Antony's servicemen remained fighting here, they were not fanning out to discover the real Brutus. But he was not prepared to see Cato suffer a mortal wound mere yards from him.

Oh, young and noble Cato, are you down? Why, now you die as bravely as Titinius, and may be honored, being Cato's son.

His reverie did not last, as he blinked to find an enemy's sword-tip inches from his face.

The soldier reached up and seized Lucilius' fighting arm.

---

[10] *There is some contention as to which character speaks these words. Some editions include them as part of Young Cato's speech; others have them spoken by Brutus himself, who then exits the stage immediately thereafter (the Yale edition does this, though they place Brutus' name in brackets and acknowledge the uncertainty in their Notes). But most editions assign this to Lucilius, based on the dialogue that soon follows. Agreeing with the Riverside and other editions, I have also assigned them to Lucilius.*

"Yield," the man snarled, "or you die."

Lucilius relaxed his stance and dropped his blade, but kept his shoulders squared. "I only yield in order *to* die; there is so much reason for my death [11] that you will kill me straight away." He held himself tall, committed to his masquerade to the end. "Kill *Brutus*, and be honored in his death."

The soldier looked very tempted indeed, but he stayed his hand. Instead, he smirked and said, "We must not." He then called out at the top of his lungs. "A noble prisoner!"

Beyond the soldier and those around him, falling friends and victorious foes, Lucilius saw Antony approaching on horseback; he ducked his head low, to maintain his charade as long as possible.

"Make room, ho!" cried another soldier near the first. "Tell Antony *Brutus* is taken."

"*I'll* tell the news," snapped the first soldier. "Here comes the General." Secure that "Brutus" was theirs, he held his sword high and called to his leader, "Brutus is taken! Brutus is taken, my lord!"

When he reached them, Antony remained mounted upon his steed as he peered about. "Where is he?"

Lucilius lifted his head then, and saw understanding in Antony's face. "*Safe*, Antony;" he answered the Triumvir, "Brutus is safe enough. I dare assure you that no enemy shall ever take the noble Brutus alive; the gods defend him from so great a shame! When you do find him – alive or dead – he will be found *like* Brutus, dictated by *himself.*"

At that, Antony actually smiled down at Lucilius, his expression one of respect, even admiration.

To the soldier who had seized Lucilius, Antony proclaimed, "This is not Brutus, friend; but I assure you, a prize no less in worth." He raised his voice so that others might hear. "Keep this man safe.

---

[11] *Some editions add a stage direction here of Lucilius offering the soldier money, treating "there is so much" as a bribe to the soldier to kill him. But, as the Yale Shakespeare argues, this makes little sense, for the soldier could loot any money Lucilius might have from his corpse; and therefore, the "there is so much" was actually meant as, "there is so much reason for my death," as I have reworded it.*

Give him all kindness. I had rather have such men my friends than enemies." To the second soldier, he ordered, "Go on, and see whether Brutus is alive or dead, and bring us word, unto Octavius' tent, how everything has chanced."

With one last look up into the hills above – why had his enemies ever abandoned such an advantageous position? – Antony guided his steed about and left the battlefield.

PART FIVE

CHAPTER FIVE

Brutus and the few remaining men in his personal guard – Dardanius, Clitus, Strato, and Volumnius – staggered further into the hills, higher even than where Cassius had fallen. They were depleted and faltering, and Brutus was no longer in denial as to their fate; darkness was falling, in all meanings.

Reaching another fair plateau, Brutus waved them to a halt. "Come, poor remains of friends," he said, "rest on this rock."

Brutus did so, and most of the others followed suit. Only Clitus stayed on his feet, peering down to the plains below; he held fast for several minutes, swaying in fatigue, until his head lowered and his shoulders drooped.

"Statilius showed the signal torchlight," he reported, "but my lord, he did not come back. He is taken, or slain."

Brutus accepted this, saying only, "Sit down, Clitus. 'Slaying' is the word; it is a deed in fashion this day."

Clitus nodded and shuffled over toward where Strato appeared to have fallen asleep. Brutus watched the man, and just before Clitus would have sat as instructed, he spoke, "Hark, Clitus."

Clitus stopped and looked to his lord.

Brutus rose and gestured for Clitus to join him in stepping away from the other men. When the two had some semblance of privacy, Brutus leaned over and whispered into Clitus' ear.

Clitus jolted and retreated a step. "What ... *I*, my lord?" He then shook his head with vehemence. "*No*, not for all the world."

Brutus nodded his understanding. "Peace, then; no words."

But Clitus still insisted, "I'll rather kill myself."

Brutus' only reply was a gentle smile of appreciation. Then he called, "Hark, Dardanius."

Dardanius, too, joined his leader for a private, whispered word, and he, too, recoiled from Brutus' request, stammering, "Shall *I* do such a deed?"

Brutus again accepted the rejection with grace and understanding, and moved off on his own, peering downhill as Clitus had done.

The two men to whom Brutus had whispered edged together for their own quiet conference.

"Oh, Dardanius!" Clitus shuddered.

"Oh, Clitus!" Dardanius breathed in return.

"What ill request did Brutus make to you?"

"To kill him, Clitus." Dardanius gestured toward the motionless Brutus, who stood in profile to them with intense angst upon his face. "Look, he meditates."

Clitus gazed at Brutus in admiration. "That noble vessel so full of grief now, it runs over even at his eyes."

Perhaps he heard them, perhaps not, but Brutus chose that moment to call out, "Come here, good Volumnius. Listen to a word."

Volumnius hurried as best he could to Brutus' side. "What says my lord?"

Brutus faced the man. "Why this, Volumnius: The ghost of Caesar has appeared to me two times by night; at Sardis once, and this last night here in Philippi fields." He paused, then nodded to himself before declaring, "I know my hour has come."

Volumnius' eyes widened. "Not so, my lord."

"No," Brutus insisted, "I am sure it is, Volumnius. You see the world, Volumnius, how it goes; our enemies have driven us to the pit." As if to prove his point, the hills echoed with another call-to-arms – said call coming, not from their own scattered forces, but from Antony's troops. Pressing forth with his metaphor, Brutus said, "It is more worthy to leap in ourselves than linger till they push us."

Volumnius looked to the sound of the approaching enemy, his eyes closing.

"Good Volumnius," Brutus pressed, "you know that we two went to school together; for that, our love of old, I please ask you: Hold my sword hilt while I run myself on it."

Brutus reached for his gladius, but Volumnius seized his wrist. "That's not an office for a friend, my lord."

Again, the enemy's call-to-arms sounded, closer than ever. Even Strato jolted awake and staggered back to his feet.

Clitus stole one peek over the edge of the plateau, then he rushed to Brutus' side. "Fly, *fly*, my lord! There is no lingering here."

But Brutus shook his head; he would fly no further. Instead, he took each of their hands as he said, "Farewell to you ... and you ... and you, Volumnius." He paused long enough to smile and add, "Strato, you have been all this while asleep. Farewell to you, too, Strato."

They all sagged upon hearing his goodbye, understanding what it meant.

Taking them all in, he said, "Countrymen, my heart does joy that, in all my life, I found no man anything but true to me. I shall have glory by this losing day – more than Octavius and Mark Antony shall attain by this vile conquest. So fare you well, all of you, for Brutus' tongue has almost ended his life's history: Night hangs upon my eyes; my bones – that have labored to attain this hour – would rest."

Below them, the closest call-to-arms yet. And someone screamed, "Fly, fly, fly!"

Clitus tried one last time. "Fly, my lord, fly!"

Brutus smiled at him once again, then withheld a sigh and spoke the words he knew Clitus longed to hear. "Go. I will follow."

Everyone present knew it would not be so, but his men appreciated this kind salve upon their wounded souls. Dardanius, Clitus, and Volumnius turned on their heels and began struggling uphill once more; Strato looked after them, back to Brutus, then after his fellow soldiers once more, wanting to leave, but not wanting to abandon Brutus, who was making no motion to retreat.

His hesitation cost him.

"I please ask you, Strato," Brutus said, "stay by your lord."

Though he had slept through Brutus' requests to each of the others, Strato could sense where this was going. But he stayed.

Brutus continued, "You are a fellow of a good reputation; your life has had some taste of honor in it." He drew his gladius from its scabbard. "Hold, then, my sword, and turn your face away while I do run upon it." He held the sword out, hilt-first. "Will you, Strato?"

Strato looked down at the sword, then took it in his grasp; but rather than turn his face away, as Brutus had offered, he reached out with his free arm. "Give me your hand first."

Moved almost to tears, Brutus accepted Strato's free hand. They faced one another, so much passing between them without speaking. All the sounds of the fighting below, closer though it must be, seemed to fade away.

Finally, Strato spoke, "Fare you well, my lord."

"Farewell, good Strato."

Their eyes remained locked. The tension held another breath, then two ...

... and then Brutus ran himself through.

He coughed, but he did not cry out. He gave one final nod of gratitude to Strato, then fell away from the blade, collapsing to his knees.

Peering up at nothing that Strato could see, Brutus whispered, "Caesar, now be still; I did not kill you with half so good a will."

Brutus laid upon the rocky earth, closed his eyes ... and breathed no more.

Strato stood over his lord, and waited.

The latest call-to-arms carried very little echo to Strato's ears, as the enemy's forces were so near. And still he waited.

Finally, he heard a voice ask, "What man is that?"

Another, familiar voice replied, "My master's man."

Turning, Strato spied Antony and Octavius approaching on foot, with Messala and Lucilius as their bound captives, and a contingent of their shared forces at their backs.

"Strato," Messala called, "where is your master?"

Strato strode forward to meet them. "Free from the bondage you are in, Messala." He dropped Brutus' sword to indicate no resistence, but when he continued, his eyes were upon Antony and Octavius. "The conquerors can make nothing but a fire of him, for Brutus alone overcame *himself*, and no other man has honor by his death."

Lucilius nodded at this appropriate conclusion to the lost battle. "And so Brutus *should* be found." Looking to the body lying beyond Strato, he added, "I thank you, Brutus, that you have proved Lucilius' saying true."

Octavius stared at Lucilius a moment, then he, too, nodded; it was not, perhaps, the denouement he had desired, but it was one he could respect. "All that served Brutus," he declared, "I will employ them." To Strato, he asked, "Fellow, will you devote your time to me?"

Strato hesitated, a flicker of hot emotion in his eyes ... then he cooled, and replied, "Aye, if Messala will recommend me to you."

Octavius glanced back. "Do so, good Messala."

First, Messala asked Strato, "How did my master die, Strato?"

"I held the sword, and he did run on it."

Messala bowed his head to Strato. With an emotional sigh, he said, "Then, Octavius, take him – that did the last service to my master – to follow you."

As this exchange had occurred, Antony had made his way past the rest to stand over Brutus' body. As the others settled their matter, they looked to him as he pointed down at Brutus and addressed them.

"This," Antony proclaimed, "was the noblest Roman of them all: All the conspirators, save only he, did what they did in *envy* of great Caesar; Brutus, alone, made himself one of them with a general honest thought for the common good of *all*. His life was gentle, and the elements so balanced in him that Nature might stand up and say to all the world, '*This* was a man!'"

Octavius and the others joined Antony. Octavius also studied the late Brutus, and said, "Let us treat him according to his virtue, with all respect and rites of burial. His bones shall lie within my tent tonight, as befits a soldier, arrayed honorably." He raised his voice. "So call the troops in the field to rest; and let's go away to share the glories of this happy day."

But they all remained a bit longer, in honor of the noble Marcus Brutus.

For Brutus' death, and that of Caius Cassius, at last concluded the tragedy of Julius Caesar.

The following literature and films were *invaluable* in my efforts to novelize *Julius Caesar*:

LITERATURE

The Riverside Shakespeare, 1974 edition*
The Yale Shakespeare, 1957 edition*
The Arden Shakespeare, 1998 edition
Asimov's Guide to Shakespeare, by Isaac Asimov
No Fear Shakespeare, by SparkNotes LLC

FILMS

**Julius Caesar*, 1953*
Directed by Joseph L. Mankiewicz,
starring Marlon Brando, James Mason, and Louis Calhern.

**Julius Caesar*, 1970*
Directed by Stuart Burge,
starring Charlton Heston, Jason Robards, and Sir John Gielgud.

Julius Caesar, 1950
Directed by David Bradley,
starring Charlton Heston, David Bradley, and Harold Tasker.

BBC Play of the Month: Julius Caesar, 1969
Directed by Alan Bridges,
starring Robert Stephens, Frank Finlay, and Maurice Denham.

ABOUT THE AUTHOR

CHRISTOPHER ANDREWS lives in California with his wife, Yvonne Isaak-Andrews, and their wonderful daughter, Arianna. In addition to his duties as stay-at-home Dad, he is always working on his next novels, and continues to work as an actor and screenwriter.

Excerpts from all of Christopher's novels can be found at www.ChristopherAndrews.com.

RISING STAR VISIONARY PRESS

continues the fine RISING STAR tradition of bringing you only the best and brightest undiscovered authors!

Explore the works of RSVP's featured author
CHRISTOPHER ANDREWS!

PANDORA'S GAME (ISBN #978-0977453528)
Games involving hypnosis and the supernatural unleash the unexpected.

DREAM PARLOR (ISBN #978-0977453535)
The novelization of the independent science-fiction film in the tradition of *1984* and *Total Recall*.

PARANORMALS (ISBN #978-0977453566)
A tale of superhuman wonder in the tradition of the *X-Men* and the *Wild Card* anthologies.

HAMLET: PRINCE OF DENMARK (ISBN #978-0977453559)
The novelization of Shakespeare's classic. Excellent for students or any fan of The Bard.

THE DARKNESS WITHIN (ISBN #978-0977453542)
A collection of disturbing short-stories. Includes "Connexion," the bridge between the *Triumvirate* novels PANDORA'S GAME and OF WOLF AND MAN.

OF WOLF AND MAN (ISBN #978-0982488201)
The **IPPY award-winning** sequel to PANDORA'S GAME.

NIGHT OF THE LIVING DEAD (ISBN #978-0982488218)
The novelization of the public domain horror classic.

PARANORMALS: WE ARE NOT ALONE (ISBN #978-0982488256)
The exciting second entry in Andrews' *Paranormals* saga.

MACBETH (ISBN #978-0982488270)
The novelization of another Shakespearean classic. Excellent for students or any fan of The Bard.

ARAKNID (ISBN #978-0982488294)
The terrifying third novel in Andrews' *Triumvirate* saga.

PARANORMALS: DARKNESS REIGNS (ISBN #978-1736198315)
The intense third entry in Andrews' *Paranormals* saga.

Available everywhere books are sold. Visit the author's website: www.ChristopherAndrews.com.

CPSIA information can be obtained
at www.ICGtesting.com
Printed in the USA
BVHW070643121122
651748BV00002B/27